M000197250

When Millions of People Disappear...

A Simple Guide to End Times Prophecy

BILL FREEMAN

Matthew 24:44

Bill Freeman

DEDICATION

To my beloved wife Sandy,
who in 1972 introduced me to
her Savior - Jesus Christ

TABLE OF CONTENTS

PREFACE

From the time I started seriously reading the Bible in 1973, one of my favorite topics has been End Times Prophecy. My favorite book of the Bible is Revelation. It is the last book of the Bible where many of these events are described in great detail. It fascinated me to read the precise descriptions of the events, key players, God's judgments, and the global conditions that would precede and follow the return of Jesus Christ.

Because the prophecies are scattered throughout the Bible as God gave various prophets pieces of prophetic information, we must consider all of them to get an accurate picture. Also, the symbolism and descriptions used by the prophets as they tried to describe future events in the language of their day can be confusing. As a result, some Christians today have little knowledge of End Times Prophecy while others believe it is irrelevant in terms of their personal relationship with the Lord and how they should live as a disciple of Christ. I believe they are missing so much that God wants them to know. In this book, I try to simplify and make these prophecies understandable. I do not believe God would have put them in His Word if He didn't want His children to understand them and prepare for them.

Fulfillment of prophecy is strong proof that the Bible is God's Word. Of all the major religions of the world, I'm not aware of any other where numerous detailed

prophecies are written down and then literally fulfilled hundreds of years later. In fact, in the nation
of Israel, the test for a prophet was 100% accuracy.

> *But the prophet who speaks a word presumptu-
> ously in My name which I have not commanded
> him to speak, or which he speaks in the name of
> other gods, that prophet shall die. You may say in
> your heart, 'How will we know the word which the
> Lord has not spoken?' When a prophet speaks in
> the name of the LORD, if the thing does not come
> about or come true, that is the thing which the
> LORD has not spoken. The prophet has spoken it
> presumptuously, you shall not be afraid of him.*
> (Deuteronomy 18:20-22)

About twenty-five percent of the Bible is related to
prophecies, and about half of those prophecies have
already been fulfilled in a literal way, often centuries
later. This gives us a strong basis for believing that
the remaining prophecies will likewise have a literal
fulfillment. In this book I'll focus on many of the
prophecies that have not yet been fulfilled.

You might call this a layman's guide to End Times
Prophecy because it is written by a layman for lay-
men. I have not had any seminary training. In 1973,
I attended a conference where the speaker chal-
lenged us to get a Bible and read it front to back. As
I did, it came alive for me. When I finished reading
it, I read through it again. I saw things and gained
new insights that I missed the first time. I have continued this practice of reading and studying the Bible from Genesis through Revelation over and over

since then. I have read numerous books and heard many insightful sermons over those fifty years, but most of my knowledge of scripture has come from reading it for myself with the aid of notes from a variety of Study Bibles, including the *Ryrie Study Bible*, the *MacArthur Study Bible*, the *ESV Study Bible*, and Dr. Thomas L. Constable's Bible study notes. These resources have been very helpful in terms of giving historical and archaeological details relative to many of the people and events discussed in the Old and New Testaments. They are also helpful in giving a literal translation of Greek and Hebrew words.

On a personal note, I have always thought it would be great to be caught up in the Rapture of the Church (where Christians are caught up to meet the Lord in the air) and not go through the dying process. After all, it will happen to some generation in the future, but it did not seem likely that it would be mine. However, my perspective has changed significantly. Knowing the end time conditions that are prophesied and seeing the rapidly changing events in the world today, I believe the stage is being set for the prophetic events to start happening in the near future. I will explain my reasoning later in this book. I have a strong sense of urgency about informing people about these prophecies. They can provide comfort and hope to Christians and help them to prepare for what might be coming soon. I also want to warn others of the coming judgments and encourage them to seriously consider their own spiritual condition in light of these prophecies.

INTRODUCTION

This book offers information and practical solutions for people who desperately need them. As is often the case, many of these people are unaware of how desperate their need is. My prayer is that the Lord will use His word to open their eyes to their need and to the solution He has provided for them through Jesus Christ.

If you are reading this book after millions of people have disappeared from all over the world, I can only imagine the emotions you must be experiencing. This guide attempts to answer these questions for you:

1) What really happened?
2) What will happen in the future?
3) How should I prepare for what's coming?

If you are reading this before the massive disappearance takes place, this guide will give you an understanding of the events prophesied in the Bible that could likely take place in the near future. If you have received Jesus Christ as your Savior and Lord and accepted the redemption that God offers to everyone, then this guide will answer the following for you:

1) What does the Bible say will take place in the future (maybe soon)?

2) How should I live my life today to be ready for these future events?

If you have rejected God's offer of salvation through Jesus Christ, or never heard of it, then the key question I will address for you is this:

1) What can I do to avoid experiencing these future events and judgments? (Answer: Turn to **Chapter 11, Section I** right now.)

The main future event that the Bible prophesies is the return of Jesus Christ, the Son of God. He will return to earth and judge all people who ever lived. Those who are judged to be righteous will spend eternity with Christ in heaven. Those who are judged to be unrighteous will spend eternity in hell, separated from God, in a continual state of torment. In this book we will learn about this judgment and how the Bible describes heaven and hell. More importantly, we will look at how God defines "righteous" versus "unrighteous" in this most important judgment.

The Bible also contains detailed prophecies of events that occur prior to His return. It will be a time of great tribulation as God pours out repeated judgments (punishments) on the earth. It will also be a time of evangelism and spiritual awakening as God offers mankind a final opportunity to acknowledge their sin, repent, and turn to Him for redemption and salvation.

This book attempts to give an organized description and timeline for these end time events. It will draw from prophecies made by the Old Testament prophets as well as those given by Jesus and the apostles in the New Testament. Because these events are described throughout the Bible, in various literary formats, there have been many interpretations of the prophecies and their meanings. I will not attempt to present or refute the various interpretations. I will simply present the Biblical prophecies in an orderly manner to the best of my understanding.

For convenience, I have written out many of the appropriate Bible passages for anyone reading this after the Rapture. (The translation that I will use is the *New American Standard Bible*, Updated Edition, copyright 1960-95 by The Lockman Foundation.)

I would encourage the reader to read Revelation and the various end time prophecies for yourself, using this guide or other resources to help you understand what is being discussed. Then you can draw your own conclusions as to what they mean. I am a firm believer in reading the Bible for yourself and not just accepting what a particular source tells you it says.

CHAPTER 1

WHY STUDY END TIMES

PROPHECY?

The question "Why should we study Biblical prophecy?" is certainly legitimate. The prophecies are scattered throughout the Bible as God gave various prophets pieces of prophetic information. We must consider all of them to get an accurate picture. Also, the symbolism and descriptions used by the prophets as they tried to describe future events in the language of their day can be confusing. So, why should we go to the trouble to study prophecies of future events? How can that benefit us today? Is there a compelling reason to take a fresh look at Biblical prophecy?

The Apostle Paul provided an answer to these questions when he first described the Rapture of the Church to the discouraged believers in Thessalonica. They were concerned for believers who had died, and Jesus had not yet returned. What will happen to those believers who pass away before His return? The Apostle Paul answers these questions:

> But we do not want you to be uninformed, brethren, about those who are asleep [believers who die before Christ returns], so that you will not grieve as do the rest who have no hope. For we believe that Jesus died and rose again, even so God will

1

bring with Him those who have fallen asleep in Jesus. For this we say to you by the word of the Lord, that we who are alive and remain until the coming of the Lord, will not precede those who have fallen asleep. For the Lord Himself will descend from heaven with a shout, with the voice of the archangel and with the trumpet of God, and the dead in Christ will rise first. Then we who are alive and remain will be caught up together with them in the clouds to meet the Lord in the air, and so we shall always be with the Lord. Therefore comfort one another with these words.
(I Thessalonians 4:13-18)

Studying and understanding prophecy COMFORTS believers and gives us HOPE. When we see the corruption and chaos in our culture and the world around us, it is easy to be hopeless and discouraged. We see people turning to alcohol, drugs, and suicide in record numbers today. As we study prophecy, believers are reminded that <u>God is still firmly in control</u>, and we are on the winning team. God prophesied long ago that these things will happen as part of His masterplan. He will assuredly punish the wicked and reward those who remain faithful to Him. This gives us courage, hope and strength to persevere in difficult times.

Paul gives another reason to study prophecy:

All scripture is inspired by God and profitable for teaching, for reproof, for correction, for training in righteousness; so that the man of God may be

adequate, equipped for every good work.
(II Timothy 3:16)

We cannot pick and choose the parts of the Bible that we want to study, believe, or obey. It is a complete package. Therefore, if we fail to learn about prophecy and prepare for future events, we will not be adequately equipped to fulfill the good works God has assigned to us.

Another verse to consider is:

God is not a man, that He should lie, nor a son of man, that He should repent; has He said, and will He not do it? or has He spoken, and will He not make it good? (Numbers 23:19)

This verse clearly states that everything God promised or prophesied in the Bible will take place just as He said it would. Too many prophecies have been literally fulfilled in exact detail in the past to believe that future prophecies will not be literally fulfilled as well. A prime example of an unbelievable prophecy is:

Therefore, the Lord Himself will give you a sign: Behold, a virgin will be with child and bear a son, and she will call His name Immanuel [God with us]. (Isaiah 7:14)

For many years people may have considered that impossible and thought it must be referring to something else that they didn't understand. Then, 700 years later, it was literally fulfilled when the virgin Mary was impregnated by the Holy Spirit, gave birth to the Son of God, and called him Jesus. We also believe that Jesus lived a sinless life, was crucified and buried, rose from the dead three days later, and then ascended bodily into heaven. The Apostle John documented these fulfillments in his book, the Gospel of John, which depicts the life and ministry of Jesus Christ. Toward the end of John's life, Jesus appeared to him and told him to write down detailed prophecies related to Jesus' second coming, which are documented in the Book of Revelation. While the timing or the sequence of the events can be difficult to interpret, we are assured by Jesus Himself that these things *"will take place".* (Revelation 1:19)

There's an interesting thing about the book of Revelation, which is the primary book of the Bible dedicated to end time prophecies (Chapters 4-22). It is the only book in the Bible that promises a blessing to the person that reads or hears the things written in it and then responds in obedience.

> *Blessed is he who reads and those who hear the words of the prophecy and heed the things which are written in it; for the time is near.*
> (Revelation 1:3)

It will be impossible for us to *"heed the things which are written in it"* if we are not aware of them or understand them. This unique promise makes it clear that God intends for us to read and study the book of Revelation, and He will enable us to understand it and heed the prophecies therein.

CHAPTER 2

THE BIG PICTURE

For reasons known only to Himself, the eternal, self-sufficient, all powerful God decided to create human beings to have a special relationship with Him. He decided to create them in His own image, which He did not do when He created angels and all the other creatures to whom He gave life. **He also decided to give them a free will; each person could choose to worship God and live according to His principles or reject God and pursue his or her own desires for pleasure, wealth, and power.** God knew from the beginning that they would all sin and not live up to His righteous standards, so He planned for His Son to one day pay the penalty for their sins and offer redemption to them all.

God created the universe and the earth for them to live on. He created Adam and Eve and placed them in the Garden of Eden. They enjoyed a personal relationship with God in a perfect environment. God gave them simple rules to live by and told them what would happen if they disobeyed. Eventually Satan deceived them, and they chose to disobey God. At that point everything changed. The earth was cursed. Adam and Eve and all their descendants would now have a sin nature, and their bodies would begin to age and die. There were many other negative results from their decision to disobey God.

A cycle began that has been repeated down through human history. God would give people a set of rules to live by in order to worship and honor Him and live an abundant life. He also told them what would happen if they chose to disobey Him and pursue other things and activities. In most cases He spoke through prophets to describe in detail the judgments that would come.

> *Surely the Lord God does nothing unless He reveals His secret counsel to His servants the prophets.* (Amos 3:7)

Still, in every generation most people chose to deny the existence of the true God. They might worship false gods while practicing all sorts of wickedness, or they might live a relatively moral life while denying the existence of God or any accountability to Him. These people are referred to as "unrighteous" (see **Righteous vs. Unrighteous** below). However, there were also people who had faith in God and chose to worship Him and live by His standards. Their choices and actions were evidence of their faith in God, which was the basis for their relationship with Him. These people are referred to as "righteous". Succeeding generations would become more and more wicked until God would bring on them the judgments that He had promised. This happened with the flood of Noah and with the nation of Israel. We see this cycle repeated throughout history with the rise and fall of nations and empires.

As we study the prophecies, we learn that this cycle will end. God will only tolerate the wickedness of mankind for so long, and then He will end it. In many Old Testament prophecies, God describes in detail events, people, and nations that He will judge "in the last days". In the New Testament, Jesus and the Apostles give detailed descriptions of cataclysmic judgments that God will pour out on the earth just before Jesus returns to establish His kingdom on earth. This time the judgments will not just apply to a specific nation or empire but to the entire world. God has given us these prophecies to give His people hope and to warn unbelievers how to escape the judgments that are coming. The Bible is clear that the cycle will end and gives details on how it will end. What it does not specify is WHEN.

In this book, I will try to pull these prophecies from the Old Testament and New Testament together in simple terms, so they will be easy to understand and follow. I will also present evidence that leads me to believe we are in "the last days," and the judgments are coming soon.

God will complete His plan by creating a new heaven and a new earth where He will dwell with the righteous people who have been redeemed from all nations and all generations.

Death and Resurrection

Throughout this book death and resurrection are mentioned frequently, so it is important that the reader understand what the Bible teaches about these processes. From the point of conception in the womb there are two components that make up a human being. The physical component of a person is called the body. It consists of all the physical aspects of the person that can be seen and touched. The body is temporal in that it changes over the span of a person's life and then decays at the point of death back into its basic elements – "dust to dust".

The immaterial component of a person is called the soul. It consists of the mind, emotions, will, logic, memories, personality, intelligence, choices, etc. that make up the unique identity of a person. This distinguishes each person from every other person that has ever lived. The soul of every person is immortal in that it will live forever. It is the soul of the person that decides whether or not to have faith in God and receive Christ as his/her Lord and Savior. Those who do so are declared by God to be "righteous" because their sins have been paid for by the death of Jesus on the cross. Those who reject God and His offer of redemption remain separated from God. They are referred to as the "unrighteous" or "wicked".

At the point of death, the soul separates from the body. The soul of a "righteous" person goes immediately into the presence of God, while the soul of the "unrighteous" person goes to Hades, or Sheol. (see

8

Righteous vs. Unrighteous below) THE SOULS OF PEOPLE WILL BE CONSCIOUS OF THEIR EXISTENCE AND THEIR SURROUNDINGS FOREVER.

The term resurrection refers to a point in time when a dead person's soul is rejoined to that person's body. Even if the body has decayed back into its basic elements, God will reconstruct those elements back into the person's original body. There are stories in the Bible of people being resurrected, such as Lazarus (John 11:1-44) and Jairus' daughter (Mark 5:35-42). These people were brought back to life but eventually died again. Jesus is the only person to die and then be resurrected with an immortal body.

The prophecies that we will discuss in this book describe future resurrections of different groups of people at different times. Their bodies will be resurrected and changed into immortal bodies and rejoined to their souls. Eventually, all people who have ever lived will be resurrected and receive immortal bodies that will live forever. The righteous will receive bodies that are suited for them to live in heaven with God. The unrighteous will receive bodies that will endure the torment of the lake of fire.

Types of Judgments

The Bible refers to two types of judgments. The first is similar to a courtroom judgment that we are familiar with, where the actions of individuals are judged. The judge decides the guilt or innocence of the individuals and determines their punishment, if appropriate. We will see examples of this type of judgment when we discuss the "Great White Throne" and "the Sheep and the Goats" judgments.

The other type of judgment describes examples of God punishing large groups of people simultaneously when their sin and wickedness get to the point that God determines to end it Himself. There are numerous examples in the Bible where God destroyed cities, such as Sodom and Gomorrah, or empires, such as the Assyrian and Babylonian empires. There is one example where God destroyed all life on earth with a flood. Prior to that judgment, He rescued righteous Noah and his family and a representative group of animals to repopulate the earth. In the future prophecies that we will discuss, God will pour out His wrath on the entire earth in several series of judgments. Once again, He will rescue righteous people from these judgments.

Righteous vs. Unrighteous

As discussed above, the Bible talks about two groups of people: the righteous and the unrighteous. It's critical to understand what distinguishes these two groups. As we discuss in Chapter 11, Section 1, all people sin against God, either through active rebellion against His standards or passive indifference to Him. Our thoughts, words, and actions are often self-centered and disobedient to God. This sin separates us from God. As an act of mercy and grace,

Jesus died an excruciating death on the cross to pay the penalty for our sin and reconcile people to God. This redemption is offered to everyone. Many receive it by faith, but many refuse it.

From the time of Adam and Eve until the Word of God was completed, God continued to reveal more information about Himself and the rules that He wanted people to live by in order to worship and honor Him and live an abundant life.

Prior to the resurrection of Jesus, righteous people expressed their faith in God by believing in Him and the revelation that He had given to them at that time, as with the patriarch Abraham:

> *For what does the Scripture say? "Abraham believed God, and it was credited to him as righteousness."* (Romans 4:3)

These righteous people are referred to as Old Testament saints or believers.

Since the resurrection of Jesus Christ, anyone who accepts His death as payment for their sins and by faith receives Jesus as their Lord and Savior is redeemed from the penalty of sin. They receive the Holy Spirit and receive eternal life with God. From the resurrection of Jesus until the Rapture of the Church (Chapter 3), everyone who receives Christ as their Savior and Lord is part of "the Church".

Those who receive Christ as their Savior and Lord after the Rapture of the Church are also righteous, but they are not part of "the Church". Many will

receive Christ during the Tribulation and be executed for their faith. These are called "Tribulation
martyrs". Millions more will receive Christ as Savior
during the Millennial Kingdom. They are also righteous and will live forever with Christ in heaven. The
names of all the righteous, from all ages, are written
in the Book of Life. These people are called "righteous", "saints", or "believers".

People who deny God and reject His offer of redemption through Christ, for whatever reason, remain
separated from God by their sin. If they die in this
condition, they will spend eternity separated from
God. These people are referred to as "unrighteous",
"wicked", or "unbelievers". It is not a description of
their character; they may have led relatively moral
lives and done many good deeds. They may have
been members of a local church, but they never repented of their sins and received Jesus as their personal Savior and Lord. People are judged to be
"righteous" or "unrighteous" based solely on whether
they had faith in God and accepted His offer of redemption through Jesus Christ or whether they rejected God and His offer of redemption.

CHAPTER 3

RAPTURE OF THE CHURCH

The Second Coming of Jesus Christ will occur in two phases. In the first phase, Jesus only returns to the clouds. He snatches His Church out of the world and takes us to live with Him in heaven. In the second phase, Jesus returns to the earth to rule as king for 1,000 years.

Before God destroyed all the people of the earth with a worldwide flood, He snatched Noah and his family and representative animals away in an ark. There is another rescue mission prophesied in scripture where Jesus pulls all of His followers out of the world to save them from the judgments that are coming on the earth prior to His return. This event is known as the Rapture (snatching away) of the Church. It was first mentioned by Jesus as He encouraged His disciples just prior to His death:

> Do not let your heart be troubled; believe in God, believe also in Me. In My Father's house are many dwelling places; if it were not so, I would have told you; for I go to prepare a place for you. If I go and prepare a place for you, I will come again and receive you to Myself, that where I am, there you may be also. (John 14:1-3)

This event was also described by the Apostle Paul:

13

For this we say to you by the word of the Lord, that we who are alive and remain until the coming of the Lord, will not precede those who have fallen asleep. [These are New Testament believers who have died before Jesus returns.] *For the Lord Himself will descend from heaven with a shout, with the voice of the archangel and with the trumpet of God, and the dead in Christ will rise first. Then we who are alive and remain will be caught up together with them in the clouds to meet the Lord in the air, and so we shall always be with the Lord.* (I Thessalonians 4:15-17)

Behold, I tell you a mystery; we will not all sleep, but we will all be changed, in a moment, in the twinkling of an eye, at the last trumpet; for the trumpet will sound, and the dead will be raised imperishable, and we will be changed. For this perishable must put on the imperishable, and this mortal must put on immortality. (I Corinthians 15:51-53)

Paul is explaining that at one moment in time those who died believing in Christ will be resurrected with immortal bodies, and the believers living at that time will disappear from the earth and will be given immortal bodies as they meet Jesus in the air. It will only be *"the dead in Christ"* who will be resurrected at that time. These are people who put their faith in Jesus after the Holy Spirit was given at Pentecost and then died before Jesus returns for His Church. Note that Jesus does not return to the earth at that time, just to the clouds. People on earth will be totally unaware of this event. They will obviously know that millions of people have suddenly disappeared all over the world, but they will have no idea what has happened.

For centuries, Christians have speculated on when this might occur. However, certain prophetic events that occur after the Rapture have not been in place to happen until now. For example, the Bible describes a seven-year period of judgment and persecution just before Jesus returns to the earth. During those seven years a very evil man (who will be inspired and empowered by Satan) will rule the world via a global government and economy. Also, the nation of Israel is featured in many of these prophecies. For 2,000 years, since 70 A.D., Israel was not a nation, and there was no political motivation or technical capability to establish a one-world government and economy. Then in 1948, Israel was reestablished as a nation and is now a leader among nations. Also, today there are powerful people with a lot of resources pushing to establish a global government and economy. The stage is being set today for the Tribulation (Chapter 5).

There is another prophecy where the Apostle Paul talks about the coming evil world ruler:

> *Let no one in any way deceive you, for it* [the Day of the Lord = God's judgments] *will not come unless the apostasy comes first, and the man of lawlessness is revealed, the son of destruction, who opposes and exalts himself above every so-called god or object of worship, so that he takes his seat*

in the temple of God, displaying himself as being
God. Do you not remember that while I was still
with you, I was telling you these things? And you
know what restrains him now, so that in his time
he will be revealed. For the mystery of lawlessness
is already at work; only he who now restrains will
do so until he is taken out of the way. Then that
lawless one will be revealed whom the Lord will
slay with the breath of His mouth and bring to an
end by the appearance of His coming; that is, the
one whose coming is in accord with the activity of
Satan, with all power and signs and false won-
ders, and with all the deception of wickedness for
those who perish, because they did not receive the
love of the truth so as to be saved.
(II Thessalonians 2:3-10)

This evil world ruler we know as the Antichrist; he is
the opposite of Jesus in every way. Paul refers to him
as "*the man of lawlessness*". In the book of Revelation, he is simply referred to as "*the Beast*". Note
that he will not be revealed to the world until "*he who
now restrains is taken out of the way.*" I believe the
restrainer is the Holy Spirit who currently indwells
Christians all over the world and is holding back the
forces of evil. At the Rapture of the Church, when
those indwelt by the Holy Spirit disappear, there will
be worldwide fear and chaos. That will be the opportunity for a charismatic leader who offers security
and prosperity to quickly rise to power, especially if
a worldwide government and economy are in place
or ready to be. Since the Antichrist does not come
onto the world stage until the Holy Spirit is removed

from the earth, the Rapture of the Church could be the next prophetic event to occur. The Bible is clear that no one will know the day or hour when the Rapture will occur, but we should be ready for it.

The Church in Heaven

In Chapter 6 we will see that the Church returns to earth with Jesus when He returns to set up His Millennial Kingdom. However, we will be in heaven with Christ for at least seven years before that event. Two significant events will take place during that time:

1. The Marriage of the Lamb

   "Hallelujah! For the Lord our God, the Almighty, reigns. Let us rejoice and be glad and give the glory to Him, for the marriage of the Lamb has come and His bride has made herself ready." It was given to her to clothe herself in fine linen, bright and clean; for the fine linen is the righteous acts of the saints. Then he said to me, "Write, 'Blessed are those who are invited to the marriage supper of the Lamb.'" And he said to me, "These are true words of God."
   (Revelation 19:6-9)

In this passage the Lamb refers to Jesus Christ, and the bride refers to His Church (those who have been Raptured). The scriptures refer elsewhere to the Church as the Bride of Christ. (Ephesians 5:25-30). Notice that she is clothed in fine linen, which *"is the righteous acts of the saints"*. This reinforces the concept that believers are in heaven because of their faith in God and His Christ, but it is the deeds or righteous acts they do in this life that bring recognition and rewards in heaven. (See **Chapter 8, Rewards for the Righteous**)

Biblical prophecies often have a near term and a future fulfillment. This passage is an example of that principle. The marriage of the Lamb will occur when Christ returns to heaven with His Church after the Rapture. However, the marriage supper of the Lamb will not occur until Christ physically returns to earth after the Tribulation and prepares to rule for 1,000 years. That is when the Tribulation martyrs and the Old Testament saints will receive their resurrected bodies and rewards for them to rule with Jesus during the Millennial Kingdom. These two groups are *"those who are invited to the marriage supper of the Lamb"*. They are not the bride but are honored guests of the Bridegroom.

2. Rewards for the Church – I Corinthians 3:10-15; II Corinthians 5:10

This topic is covered in detail in **Chapter 8 - Rewards for the Righteous**.

CHAPTER 4

JUDGMENT ON ENEMIES OF ISRAEL

There is a major battle described in the book of Ezekiel. This judgment will occur before the Tribulation, possibly before the Rapture. Rather than being a worldwide judgment, this will focus on a specific group of nations. It will demonstrate the Lord's special relationship with the nation of Israel as He personally devastates their enemies. The battle is described in great detail in Ezekiel Chapter 38 and Chapter 39:

> And the word of the LORD came to me saying, "Son of man [Ezekiel], set your face toward Gog of the land of Magog, the prince of Rosh, Meshech and Tubal, and prophesy against him and say, 'Thus says the Lord God, "Behold, I am against you, O Gog, prince of Rosh, Meshech and Tubal. I will turn you about and put hooks into your jaws, and I will bring you out, and all your army, ...Persia, Ethiopia and Put with them, all of them with shield and helmet; Gomer with all its troops, Beth-togarmah from the remote parts of the north ....After many days you will be summoned; in the latter years you will come into the land that is restored from the sword, whose inhabitants have been gathered from many nations to the mountains of Israel... 'Thus says the Lord God, "It will come about on

that day, that thoughts will come into your mind and you will devise an evil plan, and you will say, 'I will go ... against those who are at rest, that live securely, ...to capture spoil and to seize plunder, to turn your hand against the waste places which are now inhabited, and against the people who are gathered from the nations, who have acquired cattle and goods ...' (Ezekiel 38:1-12)

"Therefore prophesy, son of man, and say to Gog, 'Thus says the Lord God, "On that day when My people Israel are living securely, will you not know it? You will come from your place out of the remote parts of the north, you and many peoples with you, all of them riding on horses, a great assembly and a mighty army; and you will come up against My people Israel like a cloud to cover the land. It shall come about in the last days that I will bring you against My land, so that the nations may know Me when I am sanctified through you before their eyes, O Gog." (Ezekiel 38:14-16)

"It will come about on that day, when Gog comes against the land of Israel," declares the Lord God, "that My fury will mount up in My anger. In My zeal and in My blazing wrath I declare that on that day there will surely be a great earthquake in the land of Israel.... the mountains also will be thrown down, the steep pathways will collapse, and every wall will fall to the ground. I will call for a sword against him on all My mountains," declares the Lord God. "Every man's sword will be against his brother. With pestilence and with blood I will enter

20

into judgment with him; and I will rain on him and on his troops, and on the many peoples who are with him, a torrential rain, with hailstones, fire and brimstone. I will magnify Myself, sanctify Myself, and make Myself known in the sight of many nations, and they will know that I am the Lord."
(Ezekiel 38:18-23)

"My holy name I will make known in the midst of My people Israel; and I will not let My holy name be profaned anymore. And the nations will know that I am the Lord, the Holy One in Israel. Behold, it is coming, and it shall be done." declares the Lord God. "That is the day of which I have spoken." (Ezekiel 39:7-8)

To summarize: The Lord will bring a mighty army against Israel, and He calls them by name. The nations that are named would today include the nations of Russia, Iran, Turkey, Libya, Ethiopia and others. These nations will see Israel living securely and prosperously. They will devise a plan to conquer Israel and plunder her resources. While the nations believe this is their plan, God prophesied this battle 2,600 years ago. In reality, God will bring this mighty army against Israel in order to demonstrate His power and His special relationship with Israel. You can feel the strong emotion in the voice of the Lord in these passages. Such zeal is rarely found in Scripture. Israel will evidently not fight to defend herself. God Himself will destroy this massive army on the mountains of Israel. This battle will demonstrate to the nations, and to Israel, the awesome power of Israel's God and His strong devotion to Israel.

> And the house of Israel will know that I am the
> Lord their God from that day onward.... Therefore,
> thus says the Lord God, "Now I will restore the for-
> tunes of Jacob and have mercy on the whole house
> of Israel; and I will be jealous for My holy name.
> They will forget their disgrace and all their treach-
> ery which they perpetrated against Me, when they
> live securely on their own land with no one to make
> them afraid. When I bring them back from the peo-
> ples and gather them from the lands of their ene-
> mies, then I shall be sanctified through them in the
> sight of the many nations.... I will not hide My face
> from them any longer, for I will have poured out My
> Spirit on the house of Israel," declares the Lord
> God. (Ezekiel 39:22-29)

An interesting factor about this coming battle is that
it is not a religious war as past wars have been. This
is about resources and power: *"to capture spoil and
to seize plunder"*. The alliances are no longer Mus-
lims versus Jews but economic alliances. The recent
treaties brokered in the Middle East established
strong economic incentives for Arab nations to make
treaties with Israel. Another recent development is
that the United States is taking steps to renew the
Iran Nuclear Deal and is not likely to stand against
Iran and its allies to defend Israel. Thus, the nations
identified by Ezekiel will see this as their chance to
destroy Israel and plunder her resources, just as
God prophesied. These nations have never been

allies in the past, quite the opposite, but today they are coming together for political and economic reasons.

Just to clarify, this is not the battle of Armageddon, which occurs at the end of the seven-year tribulation, when Jesus returns to earth. In that battle, the enemy armies will be destroyed by Christ Himself. In this battle, the enemy armies are destroyed by an earthquake, torrential rain, and hailstones on the mountains of Israel.

So, when will this battle take place? Like the Rapture, there are no prophetic events that must take place before this battle occurs. Today, Israel is stronger militarily than they have been since becoming a nation, and they are very prosperous. In addition, they are signing treaties with many of their Arab neighbors. Many Arab nations are looking to Israel because they fear Iran and because they see economic advantages to aligning with Israel. Therefore, Israel is living securely in their land and are prosperous.

Another event that could push for this battle to occur in the near future is the construction of the East Med pipeline. For years Russia has been the main supplier of oil and natural gas to Europe, which has been a significant source of income for Russia. However, in recent years huge deposits of natural gas were discovered in Israel. Then in 2019, an agreement was signed between Israel, Greece, and Cyprus to build an underwater pipeline between Israel and Greece to supply natural gas to Greece and then on to Italy and all of Europe. The planning phase of this massive project is scheduled to be completed by the end of 2021. Completion of this project could have a major negative economic impact on Russia as well as significantly reducing its influence over Europe. This could be a strong incentive for Russia to join with Iran and others to invade Israel in an attempt to take control of her resources as is prophesied in Ezekiel 38 & 39. Also, securing this supply of energy to Europe, which will be ruled by the Antichrist during the Tribulation, could be an incentive for the Antichrist to sign the treaty with Israel which will start the seven-year Tribulation.

CHAPTER 5

SEVEN YEARS OF TRIBULATION

Just prior to Christ's physical return to earth there will be a seven-year period known as "The Tribulation". This was first mentioned in Daniel 9:27. The clock starts ticking when the Antichrist signs a seven-year treaty with the nation of Israel; seven years later Jesus will return to the earth.

The Bible says a great deal about this period and several individuals or groups that will play key roles during this time of tribulation. While several of the prophetic events described are sequential, many of them run concurrently.

Certain events will occur during the first 3-1/2 years as the Antichrist is consolidating his power and authority as world leader. At the midpoint of the Tribulation, the Antichrist will stop the Jewish worship of God in the temple in Jerusalem. Along with the False Prophet, he will erect a statue of himself in the temple and demand that he be worshipped as god. This is referred to as the *"Abomination of Desolation."* (Daniel 9:27 and Matthew 24:15-22). This event will initiate the second 3-1/2 years, which is called the Great Tribulation.

There may be some time between the Rapture of the Church and the beginning of the seven-year

Tribulation, and there is no indication of how long that might be. I suspect it will not be long.

I. Divine Judgments

God will pour out three series of judgments of increasing severity on the world. These judgments are not focused on individuals or nations; they are punishments affecting the whole world because wickedness and idolatry are pervasive over the entire planet. The Bible describes these series of judgments in detail, but I will only summarize them for you. These judgments will be listed in the sequence in which they are given in the Bible. They begin after the Rapture and conclude with the return of Christ at the end of the Tribulation.

A. Seal Judgments – The first series of judgments occur as Christ breaks seven seals on a scroll given to Him by God the Father. The first four are often referred to as "The Four Horsemen of the Apocalypse". (Revelation, Chapter 6)

1. *"...when the Lamb broke one of the seven seals...I looked, and behold, a white horse, and he who sat on it had a bow; and a crown was given to him, and he went out conquering and to conquer."* This refers to the Antichrist – the world ruler who will rise to power through deception and conquest.

26

He will be discussed in detail under the category of Key Figures.

2. *"When He broke the second seal, I heard the second living creature saying 'Come', and another, a red horse went out; and to him who sat on it, it was granted to take peace from the earth, and that men would slay one another; and a great sword was given to him."* This represents war on a worldwide scale.

3. *"When He broke the third seal...behold, a black horse; and he who sat on it had a pair of scales in his hand..."* This refers to famine. Worldwide war will destroy much of the world's food supply - resulting in global hunger.

4. *"When the Lamb broke the fourth seal...I looked, and behold, an ashen horse; and he who sat on it had the name Death; and Hades was following with him. Authority was given to them over a fourth of the earth, to kill with sword and with famine and with pestilence and by the wild beasts of the earth."* A fourth of the world's population will be dead from war, famine, and pestilence by this point, and the judgments are just beginning.

27

5. *"When the Lamb broke the fifth seal, I saw underneath the altar the souls of those who had been slain because of the word of God, and because of the testimony which they had maintained ..."* These are saints who came to faith in Christ after the Rapture and were martyred (killed) for their faith or for helping other believers or refusing to take the Mark of the Beast.

6. *"I looked when He broke the sixth seal, and there was a great earthquake; and the sun became black...and the whole moon became like blood; and the stars of the sky [meteors] fell to the earth.... The sky was split apart like a scroll when it is rolled up, and every mountain and island were moved out of their places. Then the kings of the earth and the great men and ... the rich and the strong and every slave and free man hid themselves in the caves and among the rocks of the mountains, and they said to the mountains and to the rocks, 'Fall on us and hide us from the presence of Him who sits on the throne, and from the wrath of the Lamb; for the great day of their wrath has come, and who is able to stand?'"* A massive earthquake will move mountains and islands and will generate volcanos that will darken the sky. While the first five seals described human activity, these describe supernatural judgments. The people of the earth will

be terrified as they realize they are experiencing the wrath of God.

7. *"When the Lamb broke the seventh seal... I saw the seven angels who stand before God, and seven trumpets were given to them.... and there followed peals of thunder and ... lightning and an earthquake. And the seven angels who had the seven trumpets prepared themselves to sound."* (Revelation 8:1-6)   The seventh seal judgment includes the following series of trumpet judgments, along with another earthquake.

B. **Trumpet Judgments** – These judgments occur during the second half of the seven-year Tribulation and are more severe than the Seal Judgments.   The first four announce divine destruction of the earth's ecology, and the final three involve demonic torment of the earth's inhabitants. (Revelation, Chapters 8-11):

1. *"The first sounded, and there came hail and fire, mixed with blood, and they were thrown to the earth; and a third of the earth was burned up, and a third of the trees were burned up, and all the green grass was burned up."* This judgment will destroy one third of the plant life all over the world.

2. *"The second angel sounded and something like a great mountain burning with fire was thrown into the sea: and a third of the sea became blood, and a third of the creatures which were in the sea and had life, died; and a third of the ships were destroyed."* This could be a huge meteor or asteroid surrounded by gases that will ignite when it enters earth's atmosphere. It will kill one-third of the sea life, and its impact will create a tidal wave to destroy one-third of the world's ships.

3. *"The third angel sounded, and a great star fell from heaven, burning like a torch, and it fell on a third of the rivers and on the springs of waters. The name of the star is called Wormwood, and a third of the waters became wormwood, and many men died from the waters, because they were made bitter."* This is possibly a comet with a fiery trail. It will disintegrate as it approaches the earth, scattering pieces all over the earth. (Wormwood is a bitter, poisonous substance that comes from the root of a plant.) Thus, this judgment will poison one-third of the fresh water on earth.

4. *"The fourth angel sounded, and a third of the sun and a third of the moon and a third of the stars were struck, so that a third of them would be darkened and the day would*

not shine for a third of it, and the night in the same way." Darkening the sun by a third will cause a severe drop in temperature and other climate change effects. It will also likely affect food crops all over the world.

5. *"Then the fifth angel sounded, and I saw a star from heaven which had fallen to the earth; and the key of the bottomless pit was given to him. He opened the bottomless pit, and smoke went up out of the pit ... out of the smoke came locusts upon the earth, and power was given them, as the scorpions of the earth have power. They were told not to hurt the grass of the earth, nor any green thing, nor any tree, but only the men who do not have the seal of God on their foreheads. And they were not permitted to kill anyone, but to torment for five months; and their torment was like the torment of a scorpion when it stings a man. And in those days men will seek death and will not find it; they will long to die, and death flees from them."* These are not ordinary locusts, but demons who will torment and terrorize people for five months. The star from heaven is likely Satan himself. The bottomless pit, also known as the abyss, is the place where the most vicious of the demons are imprisoned. *"The seal of God on their foreheads"* refers to the 144,000 Jewish evangelists discussed later under Key Figures. It's

interesting that people will not be able to commit suicide during this time.

6. *"Then the sixth angel sounded, and I heard a voice [saying].... 'Release the four angels [demons] who are bound at the great river Euphrates.' And the four angels, who had been prepared for the hour and day and month and year, were released, so that they would kill a third of mankind. The number of the armies of the horsemen was two hundred million...."* This is another demonic force that is allowed to kill one-third of the remaining population of the earth. Between the fourth seal judgment and this judgment, well over half the population of the earth (approximately 4 billion people) will have died since the Tribulation began.

After a detailed description of this demonic army, there is an interesting comment in Revelation 9:20-21: *"The rest of mankind, who were not killed by these plagues, did not repent of the works of their hands, so as not to worship demons, and the idols of gold and of silver ..., and they did not repent of their murders nor of their sorceries [drugs] nor of their immorality nor of their thefts."* Even though people will know that God is judging them, they will still refuse to submit to His authority and turn from their wicked ways.

7. *"Then the seventh angel sounded; and there were loud voices in heaven, saying, "The kingdom of the world has become the kingdom of our Lord and of His Christ; and He will reign forever and ever."* As with the seal judgments, the seventh trumpet judgment includes seven bowl judgments, along with an earthquake and a hailstorm.

C. **Bowl Judgments** – These are the most severe judgments, and they come in rapid succession at the end of the Tribulation just before Christ returns. (Revelation 16):

1. *"Then I heard a loud voice from the temple, saying to the seven angels, 'Go and pour out on the earth the seven bowls of the wrath of God.' So the first angel went and poured out his bowl on the earth; and it became a loathsome and malignant sore on the people who had the mark of the beast and who worshiped his image."* With this judgment, as with the fifth trumpet judgment, God differentiates between His followers and those who worship Antichrist.

2. *"The second angel poured out his bowl into the sea, and it became blood like that of a dead man; and every living thing in the sea*

died." All remaining sea life dies and begins to rot in the oceans.

3. "*Then the third angel poured out his bowl into the rivers and the springs of waters; and they became blood. And I heard the angel of the waters saying, 'Righteous are You, who are and who were, O Holy One, because You judged these things; for they poured out the blood of saints and prophets, and You have given them blood to drink. They deserve it.*'" Evidently, people will be able to drink this polluted water, but it will be nasty.

4. "*The fourth angel poured out his bowl upon the sun, and it was given to it to scorch men with fire. Men were scorched with fierce heat; and they blasphemed the name of God who has the power over these plagues, and they did not repent so as to give Him glory.*" Such intense heat will likely melt the polar ice caps, which could raise the level of the oceans by 200 feet. This would flood major coastal cities all over the world, contributing to additional loss of life. It could also disrupt whatever shipping still exists at that time because existing ports would be under water.

5. "*Then the fifth angel poured out his bowl on the throne of the beast, and his kingdom*

became darkened; and they gnawed their tongues because of pain, and they blasphemed the God of heaven because of their pains and their sores; and they did not repent of their deeds." Again, God distinguishes between His followers and those of Antichrist. This is like the ninth plague that occurred in Egypt (Exodus 10:21-23): *"Then the Lord said to Moses, 'Stretch out your hand toward the sky, that there may be darkness, even a darkness which may be felt.' So Moses stretched out his hand toward the sky, and there was thick darkness in all the land of Egypt for three days. They did not see one another, nor did anyone rise from his place for three days, but all the sons of Israel had light in their dwellings."*

6. *"The sixth angel poured out his bowl on the great river, the Euphrates; and its water was dried up, so that the way would be prepared for the kings from the east."* Satan will then gather the kings (nations) of the earth together at a plain north of Jerusalem called Armageddon. Some of these kings will come from the east of Israel. The Euphrates River will conveniently dry up for them.

7. *"Then the seventh angel poured out his bowl upon the air, and a loud voice came out of the temple from the throne, saying, 'It is*

done.' And there were flashes of lightning and sounds and peals of thunder; and there was a great earthquake, such as there had not been since man came to be upon the earth, so great an earthquake was it, and so mighty. The great city [Jerusalem] was split into three parts, and the cities of the nations fell... And every island fled away, and the mountains were not found. And huge hail-stones, about one hundred pounds each, came down from heaven upon men; and men blasphemed God because of the plague of the hail, because its plague was ex-tremely severe." This final judgment of a massive earthquake and giant hailstones will topple all the mountains and cause all islands to disappear. It will also destroy any remaining cities. God will change the topography of the earth to prepare for the Millennial Kingdom.

II. General Characteristics of the Tribulation

A. War – Four Horsemen

As Jesus predicted in Matthew 24:6-8, there would be numerous wars and conflicts. In the anarchy and fear following the Rapture of the Church, many ruthless leaders will attack other nations to build their kingdoms and power (the red horse of war). Because of these numerous conflicts all over the world, crops will be destroyed or not planted (the black horse of famine). The wars and famine will cause one quarter of the world's population to die (the pale horse of death).

In this climate of fear and chaos individuals and nations will give up their freedom and sovereignty to a charismatic leader who promises peace and security. The Antichrist (the rider of the white horse) will use deception to get many nations to submit to his rule. Satan will empower him also with military prowess that will enable him to conquer other nations. The Bible describes some of these wars in detail. As the judgments increase in intensity, there will be no joy or peace on the earth. People will experience panic and fear concerning what may be coming next – especially as they realize they are not just experiencing persecution from evil rulers but from the wrath of God.

B. Deception and Lawlessness

Deception on a global scale will be the norm after the Rapture.

> *Then that lawless one will be revealed whom the Lord will slay with the breath of His mouth and bring to an end by the appearance of His coming; that is, the one whose coming is in accord with the activity of Satan, with all power and signs and false wonders, and with all the deception of wickedness for those who perish, because they*

did not receive the love of the truth so as to be saved. (II Thessalonians 2:8-10)

Of course, the *"lawless one"* is the Antichrist who will be discussed further under Key Figures below. This man will be empowered by Satan with unusual power and the *"deception of wickedness"* to deceive the people who *"did not receive the love of the truth so as to be saved"*. The people who believe the truth of the Gospel after the Rapture, commit their lives to Christ, and receive eternal life will not be deceived. Everyone else will be deceived by the Antichrist.

We see this description of the Antichrist confirmed in the book of Daniel:

> *"A king will arise, insolent and skilled in intrigue. His power will be mighty, but not by his own power, and he will destroy to an extraordinary degree and prosper and perform his will; he will destroy mighty men and the holy people* [Jews]. *And through his shrewdness he will cause deceit to succeed by his influence; and he will magnify himself in his heart, and he will destroy many while they are at ease."* (Daniel 8:23-25)

This man will seduce the world by offering peace and prosperity. This is how he will conquer many of the nations that come under his rule.

In our world today, we have witnessed a rapid rise in deception. We see deception in the media, censorship in social media platforms, and other attempts to silence anyone who offers information contrary to what the powerful elite want people to believe. This has always been the case in communist countries, but now it is exploding in nations of the "free world". This is another example of the stage being set for the events that are prophesied in the Bible for the end times.

C. Global Religious System

There is much symbolism in Revelation Chapters 17 & 18, and confusion because both chapters refer to *"Babylon the Great"*. The difference is that Chapter 17 is describing the global religious system, and Chapter 18 is describing an actual city of Babylon, which we'll look at in the next topic. These prophecies are too extensive to write them out here. I would encourage you to read them for yourself after reading the explanatory notes that I offer here. Hopefully, they will help you understand the prophecies.

Chapter 17 describes a woman sitting on a scarlet beast. She is called *"Babylon the Great, the mother of harlots"*. In the Bible, harlotry or adultery is often used to symbolize idolatry. For example, when the Jews worshiped foreign gods and idols in addition to Jehovah, it was referred to as committing adultery. In this case, Babylon the Great represents the world-wide religious system that the False Prophet will establish. This religious organization amasses great wealth from her member churches all over the world. Multitudes of Christians are killed for refusing to deny Christ and join this cult. The woman sits on a scarlet beast who later turns on her and destroys her. The scarlet beast represents the Antichrist. During the first half of the Tribulation, he supports this religious movement as a means to unite the nations under his rule. At the midpoint of the Tribulation, the Antichrist puts an end to this global religious system, as well as the Jewish worship of God in their temple, and demands that the world worship him as god. The False Prophet will support him and direct that everyone worship the Antichrist. Thus, the destruction of "*Babylon the Great, the Mother of Harlots*" occurs at the midpoint of the Tribulation.

D. Global Government and Economy

In Revelation 18, Babylon the Great is referred to several times as a great city that is destroyed suddenly:

> *For this reason, in one day her plagues will come, pestilence and mourning and famine, and she will be burned up with fire; for the Lord God who judges her is strong. .... 'Woe, woe, the great city, Babylon, the strong city!*

For in one hour your judgment has come.'
(Revelation 18:8-10)

This Babylon will be a great city of unbelievable wealth and power. It may even be built on the site of ancient Babylon. It will serve as the capital of the Antichrist's empire. All the people and resources for making and enforcing laws and policies on a global scale will be located there. The Antichrist will be the leader of this government. Using the excuse of the worldwide famine, he will implement global trade policies to override any national trade policies or tariffs. Some nations will oppose the Antichrist's takeover of their country and will attempt to stop it. This will result in numerous wars that the Antichrist will win.

It will also be the center for the global economy and world trade. Many merchants and transportation magnates will become extremely wealthy as they operate global businesses from there. This will include the sale and distribution of alcohol, drugs, prostitution, and other things to satisfy the unrestrained sinful desires of people all over the world. The wealth, power, and decadence of this city will be hard to imagine.

The sudden destruction of the city comes at the end of the Great Tribulation. It may be caused by the great earthquake that occurs with the seventh bowl judgment.

E. Evangelism and Persecution of Christians

As God pours out His wrath and righteous judgments on the world, He offers grace and mercy to individuals. This is their last chance to escape eternal punishment.

> *The Lord is not slow about His promise, as some count slowness, but is patient toward you, not wishing for any to perish but for all to come to repentance.* (II Peter 3:9)

Right after the Rapture of the Church, many people will realize what just happened. Some who thought they were Christians because they went to church, lived a moral life, and helped those in need will realize they were not really believers. They had never repented of their sins, accepted Jesus' death on the cross as payment for their sins, and by faith received Jesus as their Lord and Savior. Others may have heard the Gospel message from family or friends, but they were not ready at that time to receive Christ and turn their lives over to Him. (Friend – this may be you! If so, I would encourage you to go right now to **Chapter 11, Section I** and read **Accept Jesus as Your Savior and Lord**.) Then come back and read the rest of this book. You will have greater perspective and understanding at that point.

As I mentioned, many people all over the world will realize the truth of what has happened, and they will receive Christ as their Savior.

They will sense an urgency to tell the truth to those they love and to many others. They will also want to associate with other believers. This will form the base for the Tribulation church, which will be forced to go underground because of the persecution that will soon follow. They will form an underground economy in order to survive when only those people who have the mark of the beast will be able to buy or sell anything. Also, the persecution of believers will not just come from the government. They will also be turned in to authorities by their friends and family members who have been deceived.

Throughout its history, the church of Jesus Christ has always been the strongest and expanded rapidly during times of persecution. This will be the case in the Tribulation. As in past times of persecution, many believers will be imprisoned and/or martyred, but they will immediately experience eternal life with Christ upon their deaths.

As we will see next, to assist the Tribulation church in spreading the gospel around the world, God will provide special witnesses and evangelists during this time.

III. Key Figures

A. 144,000 Jewish Evangelists – Revelation 7:1-8; Revelation 14:1-5

After the sixth Seal judgment, but before the seventh, there is an interlude where a hush comes over the whole earth. No wind blows anywhere on the planet. At that time, 144,000 Jews (12,000 from each of the twelve tribes of Israel) are sealed with the mark of God on their foreheads. These special redeemed Jews will take the Gospel message to Jews and Gentiles all over the world throughout the second half of the Tribulation bringing many to salvation. God's mark will protect them from any harm as they carry out their mission.

B. Two Witnesses

And I will grant authority to my two witnesses, and they will prophesy for twelve hundred and sixty days, clothed in sackcloth.... And if anyone wants to harm them, fire flows out of their mouth and devours their enemies; so if anyone wants to harm them, he must be killed in this way. These have the power to shut up the sky, so that rain will not fall during the days of their prophesying; and they have power over the waters to turn them to blood, and to strike the earth with every plague, as often as they desire.

*When they have finished their testimony,
the beast that comes up out of the abyss* [the
Antichrist] *will make war with them and
overcome them and kill them.   And their
dead bodies will lie in the street of the great
city* [Jerusalem] *... where also their Lord
was crucified...And those who dwell on the
earth will rejoice over them and celebrate;
and they will send gifts to one another, because these two prophets tormented those
who dwell on the earth.*

*But after the three and a half days, the
breath of life from God came into them, and
they stood on their feet; and great fear fell
upon those who were watching them. And
they heard a loud voice from heaven saying
to them, "Come up here." Then they went up
into heaven in the cloud, and their enemies
watched them. And in that hour there was a
great earthquake, and a tenth of the city fell;
seven thousand people were killed in the
earthquake, and the rest were terrified and
gave glory to the God of heaven."*
(Revelation 11:3-13)

This prophecy is pretty clear. At the midpoint
of the Tribulation two prophetic witnesses will
appear in Jerusalem. They will proclaim to the
nation of Israel and the world a message of
God's judgment and His gracious offer of salvation to all who repent and receive Christ as
their Savior. They will preach for 3-1/2 years

until the end of the Tribulation. Notice that they will prophesy for *"twelve hundred and sixty days"*. Like so many prophecies, exact details are given to let us know this will be literally fulfilled.

In addition to warning the nations to repent, they have the power to hold back the rain and call down all manner of plagues on the kingdom of the Antichrist as often as they like. If anyone tries to harm them, *"fire comes out of their mouths"* to kill that person. At the end of the Tribulation, the Antichrist will be allowed to kill them. Their dead bodies will be left on the streets of Jerusalem for 3-1/2 days while the whole world celebrates their death. At the end of the 3-1/2 days, God will bring them back to life. They will stand on their feet and then rise up to heaven as their terrified enemies watch. Then a great earthquake will strike Jerusalem, destroying one-tenth of the city and killing seven thousand people.

C. Angelic Witness

During the second half of the Tribulation, God sends an angel to warn the people of the earth to turn from worshipping the Antichrist to worshipping God:

> *And I saw another angel flying in midheaven, having an eternal gospel to preach to those who live on the earth, and to every nation and tribe and tongue and people; and*

> *he said with a loud voice, "Fear God, and give Him glory, because the hour of His judgment has come; worship Him who made the heaven and the earth and sea and springs of waters." (Revelation 14:6-7)*

"Midheaven" denotes the highest and brightest point of the sun in the sky at noonday, where everyone on earth will be able to see and hear this angelic messenger. Even at this late hour God is graciously offering the people of the earth an opportunity to turn from worshipping the Antichrist and receive the salvation that He offers in Christ.

D. Satan (the Dragon)

The dragon is mentioned throughout the Book of Revelation. Satan will be allowed to exercise great power and authority and destruction during this seven-year period of Tribulation. Of course, God sovereignly limits Satan at all times.

E. Antichrist (the Beast)

This is the key human figure in the seven-year Tribulation. In the literary language of Revelation, he is called the Beast (literally "monster").

> *And the dragon stood on the sand of the seashore. Then I saw a beast coming up out of the sea...And the dragon gave him his power and his throne and great authority. I*

saw one of his heads as if it had been slain, and his fatal wound was healed. And the whole earth was amazed and followed after the beast; they worshipped the dragon because he gave his authority to the beast; and they worshipped the beast, saying, "Who is like the beast, and who is able to wage war with him?" There was given to him a mouth speaking arrogant words and blasphemies, and authority to act for forty-two months was given to him. And he opened his mouth in blasphemies against God, to blaspheme His name and His tabernacle ... It was also given to him to make war with the saints and to overcome them, and authority over every tribe and people and tongue and nation was given to him. All who dwell on the earth will worship him, everyone whose name has not been written from the foundation of the world in the book of life of the Lamb who has been slain. (Revelation 13:1-8)

Satan gives the Antichrist great powers of deception and abilities to conquer nations by war and by cunning. He will have a head wound that appears to be fatal, but he recovers – thus mimicking the resurrection of Christ. Notice however that God is still firmly in control. Wherever we read "*It was given to him...*", this is given to him by God for His purposes. The Antichrist will be given forty-two months to rule the world. This is the last half of the

Tribulation when he rules the entire world. God also allows him to blaspheme God Himself and kill many of God's faithful followers.

During the first 3-1/2 years of the Tribulation the Antichrist presents himself as a peaceful leader who wants to establish world peace and prosperity out of the global chaos that is occurring. His power base is a ten-nation confederation of nations in Europe. He subdues three of the nations; then the other seven nations submit to his authority. There will be numerous wars as many nations resist giving up their sovereignty, but Satan enables (and God allows) the Antichrist to be victorious. Remember, the rider of the white horse is a conqueror as well as a deceiver.

By the midpoint of the Tribulation, the Antichrist will have established himself as the political and economic ruler of the world, although some nations will still struggle to remain independent. At that time, he will declare himself to be god and demand that everyone worship him. Then he will reveal himself as a very ruthless world ruler.

At the end of the Tribulation, the people of the earth will see Jesus returning from heaven. The Antichrist will coordinate the armies of the earth to fight against Him in the Battle of Armageddon, but Jesus will annihilate them. The Antichrist will then be thrown alive into the lake of fire where he will live forever in torment.

F. The False Prophet (Another Beast)

Then I saw another beast coming up out of the earth; and he had two horns like a lamb, and he spoke as a dragon. He exercises all the authority of the first beast in his presence. And he makes the earth and those who dwell in it to worship the first beast, whose fatal wound was healed. He performs great signs, so that he even makes fire come down out of heaven to the earth in the presence of men. And he deceives those who dwell on the earth because of the signs which it was given him to perform in the presence of the beast, telling those who dwell on the earth to make an image to the beast who had the wound of the sword and has come to life. And it was given to him to give breath to the image of the beast, so that the image of the beast would even speak and cause as many as do not worship the image of the beast to be killed. And he causes all, the small and the great, and the rich and the poor, and the free men and the slaves, to be given a mark on their right hand or on their forehead, and he provides that no one will be able to buy or to sell, except the one who has the mark...
(Revelation 13:11-18)

This man will also be empowered and controlled by Satan and have broad powers of deception. He will appear to be gentle and religious, but he will speak the doctrines of Satan, the originator of all false religions. He is not as powerful as the Antichrist but performs miracles in his presence. While the Antichrist is primarily a political and military leader, the False Prophet is a religious leader. During the first half of the Tribulation, he will work to establish a worldwide religious system. Christians who are faithful to the God of the Bible will refuse to join this cult and will be persecuted or killed for their faith. The False Prophet will also be able to call down fire from heaven and do other miracles.

At the midpoint of the Tribulation, when the Antichrist abolishes this worldwide religious system and demands to be worshipped, the False Prophet will erect a statue of the Antichrist in the temple in Jerusalem. He will be able to animate the statue, so it appears to speak. He will then direct all of his followers to worship the Antichrist as their god. He will also direct that anyone who refuses to worship the statue should be killed.

The False Prophet is also the one who directs that everyone on earth must receive a mark on their right hand or forehead in order to buy or sell anything. This will identify a person as a worshiper of Antichrist. The Bible refers to

51

this identification number as "The Mark of the Beast" and gives a strong warning against receiving this mark, even though this will lead to hardship, persecution, and possibly execution. (Revelation 14:9-11). When Christ returns, the False Prophet will be thrown alive into the lake of fire, along with the Antichrist.

F. The Nation of Israel

The seven-year Tribulation period begins when Israel signs a seven-year treaty with the Antichrist and the European confederation of nations he leads. He will present himself as a friend and protector of Israel. At the midpoint of the seven-years, the Antichrist will forbid the Jews from worshipping their God, set up an image of himself in the temple, and demand that the Jews and everyone else worship Him as god. Jesus described this event in Matthew 24:15-22 as the *"Abomination of Desolation"*. When this occurs, Jesus warned the Jews to flee to the mountains of Israel. God will provide a sanctuary for them in the wilderness around Jerusalem.

There will be a great persecution of the Jews all over the world during the second half of the Tribulation. This is known in scripture as "the time of Jacob's trouble". This will complete the persecution of the Jewish nation that God has allowed to continue for centuries because of their idolatry and their rejection of Jesus as their promised Messiah. In many of the Old

Testament prophecies, God told the nation of Israel that they would be dispersed among the nations and persecuted because of their disobedience, but He always promised to bring them back to the land and bless them. He always professed His love and devotion to them as His chosen people. This is confirmed by the prophet Zechariah:

> *I will pour out on the house of David and on the inhabitants of Jerusalem, the Spirit of grace and of supplication, so that they will look on Me whom they have pierced; and they will mourn for Him, as one mourns for an only son, and they will weep bitterly over Him like the bitter weeping over a firstborn.* (Zechariah 12:10)

This is confirmed in the New Testament by the Apostle Paul:

> *For I do not want you, brethren, to be uninformed of this mystery – so that you will not be wise in your own estimation – that a partial hardening has happened to Israel until the fullness of the Gentiles has come in; and so all Israel will be saved; just as it is written, "The Deliverer will come from Zion, and He will remove ungodliness from Jacob." "This is My covenant with them, when I take away their sins."* (Romans 11:25-26)

God has not given up on the Jewish nation. He refers to them throughout the scripture as His beloved, His chosen people. The Lord made an everlasting covenant with Abraham:

> *"And I will make you a great nation, and I will bless you, and make your name great; and so you shall be a blessing; and I will bless those who bless you, and the one who curses you I will curse. And in you all the families of the earth will be blessed."*
> (Genesis 12:2-3)

All of the Jews who are alive at the end of the Tribulation will realize that Jesus is indeed their promised Messiah and will receive Him as their Savior and Lord.

IV. Why Would a Loving God Inflict Such Pain and Suffering?

The successive judgments of the Tribulation are a powerful display of God's justice and His righteousness. They are also a display of His mercy and lovingkindness. He knows that everyone who dies without repenting of their sins and receiving the redemption that is offered in Christ, will spend eternity in torment in the lake of fire. This grieves the heart of God. He declares this to the prophet Ezekiel:

> *Say to them, 'As I live!' declares the Lord God, 'I take no pleasure in the death of the wicked,*

but rather that the wicked turn from his way and live. Turn back, turn back from your evil ways!' (Ezekiel 33:11)

This is confirmed by the Apostle Peter:

The Lord is not slow about His promise, as some count slowness, but is patient toward you, not wishing for any to perish but for all to come to repentance. (II Peter 3:9)

God knows the power that sin has in our lives and that each person is unique. Some people will repent and turn to God for salvation when they hear the Gospel message. Many of these people will have accepted Christ as their Savior prior to the Rapture and will escape the Tribulation judgments. Other people will have to experience the increasing pain and suffering of the Tribulation judgments before they will repent of their sins, turn to God, and by faith receive Jesus as their Lord and Savior.

God knows that this is the last chance people will have to turn to Him from their sin in order to spend eternity with Him in heaven rather than in torment in hell. Whatever pain and suffering it takes for a person to turn to God will be worth it.

As we read in previous passages, most people during the Tribulation will continue to worship and serve the Antichrist and Satan. They will die in their sins, separated from God, and spend eternity in the lake of fire with Satan and the demons. For the rest of eternity, they will remember the chances they had to turn to God but refused to do so. But what about those who did respond to God's repeated offers of mercy during the Tribulation?

> *After these things I looked and behold, a great multitude which no one could count, from every nation and all tribes and peoples and tongues, standing before the throne and before the Lamb, clothed in white robes, and palm branches were in their hands; and they cry out with a loud voice, saying "Salvation to our God who sits on the throne, and to the Lamb." ... Then one of the elders ... said to me, "These are the ones who come out of the great tribulation, and they have washed their robes and made them white in the blood of the Lamb. For this reason, they are before the throne of God; and they serve Him day and night in His temple; ... They will hunger no longer, nor thirst anymore; nor will the sun beat down on them, nor any heat; for the Lamb in the center of the throne will be their shepherd and will guide them to springs of the water of life; and God will wipe every tear from their eyes."* (Revelation 7:9-17)

This great multitude of people will be eternally grateful that God subjected them to temporary suffering in the Tribulation, so they could experience the eternal joy of living in heaven with Jesus.

CHAPTER 6

RETURN OF THE KING

The return of Jesus Christ to the earth, which is often referred to as "The Second Coming," is one of the most discussed, speculated on, and written about events in history. The birth, life, death, and resurrection of Jesus two thousand years ago is easily the most impactful event in human history. His promised return to earth will end human history as we know it.

While no one knows the day or hour when Jesus will return in the clouds to rescue His Church from the coming judgments (see **Rapture of the Church**), people living during the Tribulaton will be able to determine the date of His Second Coming to the earth. It will occur exactly seven years after the Antichrist signs a treaty with the nation of Israel.

One of my favorite scripture passages is:

> ...but let him who boasts boast of this, that he understands and knows Me, that I am the Lord who exercises lovingkindness, justice and righteousness on earth; for I delight in these things, declares the Lord. (Jeremiah 9:24)

When Jesus came the first time, He came in the role of a humble servant:

...the Son of Man did not come to be served, but to serve, and to give His life a ransom for many. (Matthew 20:28)

His life, His sacrificial death, and His resurrection made it possible for us to have redemption and eternal life with Him. This was the ultimate expression of God's lovingkindness.

When Jesus returns, He will come as the sovereign King of the universe He created. He will execute justice and righteousness on the earth. He will come in the power and glory that has been His for all eternity, and He will demonstrate that:

It is a terrifying thing to fall into the hands of the living God. (Hebrews 10:31)

Jesus described His return to His disciples:

But immediately after the tribulation of those days the sun will be darkened, and the moon will not give its light, and the stars will fall from the sky, and the powers of the heavens will be shaken. And then the sign of the Son of Man will appear in the sky, and then all the tribes of the earth will mourn, and they will see the Son of Man coming on the clouds of the sky with power and great glory. And He will send forth His angels with a great trumpet and they will gather together His elect from the four winds, from one end of the sky to the other. (Matthew 24:29-31)

A detailed description of Christ's return is also prophesied in the book of Revelation:

And I saw heaven opened, and behold, a white horse, and He who sat on it is called Faithful and True, and in righteousness He judges and wages war. His eyes are a flame of fire, and on His head are many diadems [crowns]; and He has a name written on Him which no one knows except Himself. He is clothed with a robe dipped in blood, and His name is called The Word of God. And the armies which are in heaven, clothed in fine linen, white and clean were following Him on white horses. From His mouth comes a sharp sword, so that with it He may strike down the nations, and He will rule them with a rod of iron; and He treads the wine press of the fierce wrath of God, the Almighty. And on His robe and on His thigh He has a name written, "KING OF KINGS, AND LORD OF LORDS".... And I saw the beast and the kings of the earth and their armies assembled to make war against Him who sat on the horse and against His army. And the beast was seized and with him the false prophet who performed the signs in his presence, by which he deceived those who had received the mark of the beast and those who worshipped his image; these two were thrown alive into the lake of fire which burns with brimstone. And the rest were killed with the sword which came from the mouth of Him who sat on the horse, and all the birds were filled with their flesh. (Revelation 19:11-21)

At the end of the Tribulation, Jesus will return to earth as its rightful king. He will be followed by *"the armies which are in heaven"* on white horses. This group will include New Testament saints who were gathered in the Rapture and some angels. Note that this army does not carry weapons. We will not fight in the coming battle; rather, we will rule the nations with Christ during His thousand-year reign.

As He is approaching earth, Jesus will send His angels to gather His elect from all over the world. The only believers on earth at that time will be those who are still alive at the end of the Tribulation. Apparently, this will be a secondary gathering of believers, but they will not be given immortal bodies at that time. (see **Judgment of the Sheep and the Goats**) After the removal of the living believers, only those who rejected Jesus will remain alive on the earth.

The people on earth will probably see a bright light coming toward earth as Jesus is enveloped in His divine glory. His coming will not be instantaneous this time. Since *"all the tribes of the earth"* will see Him coming, and the Antichrist will have time to organize the armies of the world to repel this apparent invasion from outer space, there may be several days that the people of the earth see Christ and His army approaching from heaven. By that point, the severe judgments of the final days of the Tribulation will have killed most of the world's population. People will be living in absolute terror.

As Jesus approaches the earth, the Antichrist assembles the armies of the world to fight against Him. The battle takes place in the plains outside of Jerusalem. This battle is commonly called the Battle of Armageddon:

...for they are spirits of demons, performing signs, which go out to the kings of the whole world, to gather them together for the war of the great day of God, the Almighty... And they gathered them together to the place which in Hebrew is called Har-Magedon [Armageddon]. (Revelation 16:14-16)

Revelation 14:20 and Revelation 19:15 indicate that it is a bloodbath as the armies are destroyed by the sword that comes from the mouth of Jesus. The Antichrist and the False Prophet will be seized and thrown alive into the lake of fire where they will be tormented forever.

Satan and his demonic forces will be imprisoned in the abyss for a thousand years. They will not be allowed to tempt mankind during the thousand-year reign of Christ. The abyss is the place where the worst demons are held captive awaiting their final judgment in the lake of fire:

Then I saw an angel coming down from heaven, holding the key of the abyss and a great chain in his hand. And he laid hold of the dragon, the serpent of old, who is the devil and Satan, and bound him for a thousand years; and he threw him into the abyss, and shut it and sealed it over him, so that he would not deceive the nations any longer, until the thousand years were completed; after these things he must be released for a short time. (Revelation 20:1-3)

Then believers who were killed during the Tribulation will be resurrected so that they can reign with

Christ for a thousand years. It will be at this time that they will receive their immortal bodies and rewards as they enter the Millennial Kingdom.

> *... And I saw the souls of those who had been beheaded because of their testimony of Jesus and because of the word of God, and those who had not worshiped the beast or his image and had not received the mark on their forehead and on their hand; and they came to life and reigned with Christ for a thousand years.* (Revelation 20:4)

It will also be at this time that the Old Testament believers will be resurrected and receive their immortal bodies and rewards. (Daniel 12:2) They will also reign with Christ in His millennial kingdom.

Judgment of the Sheep and the Goats

The last group to be dealt with before the thousand-year reign of Christ begins is the people who are alive at the end of the Tribulation. The purpose of this judgment is to decide whom Jesus will permit into His kingdom. Jesus describes this judgment as follows:

> *"But when the Son of Man comes in His glory, and all the angels with Him, then He will sit on His glorious throne. All the nations will be gathered before Him; and He will separate them from one another, as the shepherd separates the sheep from the goats; and He will put the sheep on His right, and the goats on the left.*

"Then the King will say to those on His right, 'Come, you who are blessed of My Father, inherit the kingdom prepared for you from the foundation of the world. For I was hungry, and you gave Me something to eat; I was thirsty, and you gave Me something to drink; I was a stranger, and you invited Me in; naked, and you clothed Me, I was sick, and you visited Me; I was in prison, and you came to Me.' Then the righteous will answer him, 'Lord, when did we see You hungry, and feed You, or thirsty, and give You something to drink? And when did we see You a stranger, and invite You in, or naked, and clothe you? When did we see You sick, or in prison, and come to You?' The King will answer and say to them, 'Truly I say to you, to the extent that you did it to one of these brothers of Mine, even the least of them, you did it to Me.'

"Then He will also say to those on His left, 'Depart from Me, accursed ones, into the eternal fire which has been prepared for the devil and his angels; for I was hungry, and you gave Me nothing to eat; I was thirsty, and you gave Me nothing to drink; I was a stranger, and you did not invite Me in; naked, and you did not clothe Me; sick, and in prison, and you did not visit Me.' Then they themselves also will answer, 'Lord, when did we see You hungry, or thirsty, or a stranger, or naked, or sick, or in prison, and did not take care of You?' Then He will answer them, 'Truly I say to you, to the extent that you did not do it to one of the least of these, you did not do it to Me.' These will go away into eternal punishment, but the righteous into eternal life." (Matthew 25:31-46)

Jesus describes the sheep as *"the righteous"*; these are believers who by faith accepted Christ as their savior during the Tribulation. They will be invited into the Millennial Kingdom based on how they treated *"these brothers of mine, even the least of them..."*. These *"brothers"* refer to other believers in Christ (both Jew and Gentile), including the 144,000 Jewish evangelists. To give aid or shelter to such people during the Great Tribulation meant imprisonment and probably death. The sheep took these risks and helped Christ's *"brothers"*. Note, their acts of comforting them did not earn salvation for the sheep, but their deeds were evidence of their faith in Christ, which is the basis for their being judged as *"righteous"*. These believers will enter the Millennial Kingdom alive. They will have children and grandchildren (with sin natures as they have) and begin the process of repopulating the earth.

The goats are the wicked (unrighteous) people who refused to aide Jesus' followers during the Great Tribulation. On the contrary, they were most likely persecuting and imprisoning believers in Christ. Again, their deeds reveal the rebellion in their hearts against God. The bodies of these wicked people will be killed, and their souls will be sent to Hades where they will await final judgment at the end of the Millennial Kingdom.

Now that the King has returned and judged all of the rebellious people and angels, it is time to establish the ideal kingdom for His faithful followers to live in for a thousand years.

CHAPTER 7

MILLENNIAL KINGDOM

After Jesus returns and deals with all the evil and wickedness on the earth, including imprisoning Satan and his demons for 1,000 years, He will establish His kingdom on earth. It is referred to as the "Millennial Kingdom" because it will last for a thousand years. It will be an ideal place to live in every way:

And it will come about in the last days that the mountain of the house of the LORD [the Temple mount in Jerusalem] will be established as the chief of the mountains. It will be raised above the hills, and the peoples will stream to it. Many nations will come and say, "Come and let us go up to the mountain of the LORD and to the house of the God of Jacob, that He may teach us about His ways and that we may walk in His paths." For from Zion will go forth the law, even the word of the LORD from Jerusalem. And He will judge between many peoples and render decisions for mighty, distant nations. Then they will hammer their swords into plowshares and their spears into pruning hooks; Nation will not lift up sword against nation, and never again will they train for war. Each of them will sit under his vine and under his fig tree, with no one to make them afraid, for the mouth of the LORD of hosts has spoken." (Micah 4:1-4)

The most extensive description of the Millennial Kingdom is found in the book of Ezekiel. We find there very detailed descriptions, including: 1) the new temple in Jerusalem (Chapters 40-43), 2) the new system of worship and sacrifices (Chapters 43-46), and 3) the new apportionment of the land promised to Israel (Chapters 47-48). These prophecies are given in such exact detail that it is highly unlikely they will not be fulfilled literally.

I. Natural State of the Earth

The topography of the earth will be different than it is today due to the extreme judgments during the Tribulation. The massive earthquake of the seventh bowl judgment will cause the mountains to be flattened. I suspect the ocean depths will also have been filled to some extent by underwater volcanos. The result will likely be a much more level earth surface suitable for agriculture or development. The scorching heat of the sun at the fourth bowl judgment will probably have melted the polar ice caps. It may have also regenerated (speculation on my part) the water vapor canopy that originally encircled the earth above the atmosphere that we breathe. (Genesis 1:6-8) This original canopy was the source for the forty days of rain during the flood of Noah. Such a vapor canopy would once again eliminate deserts, provide a moist greenhouse effect, and provide a temperate climate for growing crops all year long all over the earth. It would also extend life by reducing UV light waves. This is the reason people lived for hundreds of years before the flood.

The biggest change will be that God will remove the curse He placed on the earth and people after Adam and Eve sinned:

> *To the woman He said, "I will greatly multiply Your pain in childbirth. In pain you will bring forth children; yet your desire will be for your husband, and he will rule over you."*

> *Then to Adam He said, "Because you have listened to the voice of your wife and have eaten from the tree about which I commanded you, saying, 'You shall not eat from it'; cursed is the ground because of you; in toil you will eat of it all the days of your life. Both thorns and thistles it shall grow for you; and you will eat the plants of the field. By the sweat of your face you will eat bread, till you return to the ground, because from it you were taken. For you are dust, and to dust you shall return."*
> (Genesis 3:16-19)

The consequences of Adam and Eve's rebellion against God included: 1) Women would have great pain in childbirth. 2) There would be conflict and strife in their marriage relationship. 3) The ground was cursed so that it would produce thorns and thistles as well as crops. Man would have to work hard to provide for his family. and 4) Physical aging and death came upon the human race. In Romans 8:18-23, the Apostle Paul explains that all of creation was affected by the sin of Adam and Eve.

When Christ establishes His kingdom on earth, He will remove the curse on creation. The earth will once again be very productive with an abundance of crops. Another aspect of removing the curse will be a population explosion. Women will no longer have great pain in childbirth. Also, since people will not experience physical aging or natural death, they will be able to continue having children for hundreds of years. It will be possible for a woman to be pregnant at the same time her great granddaughter is pregnant. There will also not be any diseases; so, everyone will be extremely healthy.

When God created Adam and Eve, He gave them an assignment:

> *God created man in His own image, in the image of God He created him; male and female He created them. God blessed them; and God said to them, "Be fruitful and multiply, and fill the earth, and subdue it; and rule over the fish of the sea and over the birds of the sky and over every living thing that moves on the earth."* (Genesis 1:27-28)

After the flood, God gave Noah's family the same command:

> *And God blessed Noah and his sons and said to them, "Be fruitful and multiply and fill the earth.* (Genesis 9:1)

Mankind has never completed this primary assignment that God gave us. When Jesus is ruling the world as its king, people, animals, and crops will be very productive. Mankind will have another opportunity to multiply and fill the earth. It will be amazing.

One thing to remember is that everyone living on the earth at that time will still have a sin nature. They will experience pride, greed, envy, anger, jealousy, lust, and all the internal temptations that we experience today. While the first generation entering the Kingdom will all be believers, each of their descendants will have to decide for themselves whether to accept or reject Christ as Lord of their life. Many will, but many will not. Even though Satan is not tempting them, and they live a prosperous life in an ideal society, many will still rebel against God in their hearts. Even though their bodies will not age or die of natural causes, they can still die. (See Isaiah 65:20)

Also, wild animals and mankind will no longer hunt and kill one another; animals will all be vegetarians as they were before the flood:

> *Then a shoot will spring from the stem of* Jesse, [The Messiah will be a descendent of King David.] *And a branch from his roots will bear fruit. The Spirit of the LORD will rest on Him, the spirit of wisdom and understanding, the spirit of counsel and strength, the spirit of knowledge and the fear of the LORD. And He*

will delight in the fear of the LORD, and He will not judge by what His eyes see, nor make a decision by what His ears hear; But with righteousness He will judge the poor and decide with fairness for the afflicted of the earth; and He will strike the earth with the rod of His mouth, and with the breath of His lips He will slay the wicked. Also, righteousness will be the belt about His loins, and faithfulness the belt about His waist.

And the wolf will dwell with the lamb, and the leopard will lie down with the young goat, and the calf and the young lion and the fatling together; and a little boy will lead them. Also the cow and the bear will graze, their young will lie down together, and the lion will eat straw like the ox. The nursing child will play by the hole of the cobra, and the weaned child will put his hand on the viper's den. They will not hurt or destroy in all My holy mountain, for the earth will be full of the knowledge of the LORD as the waters cover the sea.
(Isaiah 11:1-9)

II. Government of the Kingdom

Jesus will rule as King over the whole world. The population around the world will still be organized into nations and governed accordingly. Jesus will establish one system of laws and religion and taxation and rules for society to live by in all the nations. All levels of leadership in government, in churches, and in courts will be filled by Old Testament and New Testament saints who have been resurrected and have glorified bodies, with no sin nature. Jesus will personally appoint each of us to the role He wants us to perform in His kingdom. This may be one of the rewards we receive when our deeds are judged (see **Rewards for the Righteous**). For example, Jesus promised His disciples that they would rule over the twelve tribes of Israel. (Matthew 19:28) There will not be any corrupt political leaders or judges or priests in the Kingdom. Each one will make decisions with complete knowledge and understanding of how Jesus wants them to rule. Each judge or other official will have immediate access to Jesus for consultation.

In addition to the above quote from Isaiah 11:1-9, we also read:

> *"From His mouth comes a sharp sword, so that with it He may strike down the nations, and He will rule them with a rod of iron..."*
> (Revelation 19:15)

Psalm 2:5 and Revelation 12:5 also refer to the Messiah as ruling with *"a rod of iron"*. This indicates that there will be no lawlessness in His kingdom because justice will be swift and certain. As we read in Isaiah 11:3-4 above: Jesus *"will not judge by what His eyes see, nor make a decision by what His ears hear..."* He will not have to see evidence or listen to testimonies relative to a crime. Because He is God, Jesus will know exactly what happened, exactly what each person said and did and what was in the heart of each person involved. Every judge will have access to this information and understanding and will be able to determine guilt or innocence immediately and the appropriate penalty when necessary.

If we look at the Mosaic Law which God gave to the nation of Israel, we can get an idea of what the legal system might look like under King Jesus. For example, under the Law if it was a crime involving property, such as theft or negligent destruction, the guilty person had to restore multiples of the property stolen or damaged to the offended person. If it was a crime against a person, such as assault or murder or adultery, the guilty person may have been put to death or required to work for the injured person without pay for a period of time. If it was a crime against God, such as idolatry or witchcraft or falsely claiming to be a prophet of God, the punishment was death. Another important aspect of the Law was that the penalty was determined by God and was known by the offender before the crime was committed.

Since punishment will be swift and sure, there will be very little crime. Think about it, if you knew for sure that if you stole something you would be quickly caught, convicted, and then have to give your victim three times as much as you had stolen; or if you murdered someone, you would be quickly put to death, would you commit the crime? Exactly – there will be very little crime throughout the 1,000 years. Many people may be rebellious in their hearts, but they will obey the law because of the certainty of swift punishment.

III. Jerusalem and the Nation of Israel

There are numerous prophecies in the Bible concerning the nation of Israel and the city of Jerusalem during the Millennial Kingdom. As I mentioned earlier, the most extensive description is given in Ezekiel, Chapters 40-48. These passages describe in great detail how the city of Jerusalem and the nation will be laid out and how God will regather the Jews from the nations where they have been dispersed and bring them back to Israel. All of the promises that God has made to Israel in the past will be fulfilled in the Kingdom.

God will enlarge the borders of Israel to include all the territory that He promised to them in the Abrahamic Covenant, which they have never possessed. The land will be apportioned to the twelve tribes of Israel. There will be a large portion of land in the center of Israel designated as the Holy District. In its center will be the rebuilt temple. The Temple Mount will have been raised up and enlarged by the final earthquake, and the temple area will be laid out as a square, measuring about one mile on each side. In the Holy District will also be land for the priests, the "Prince" who will be the administrator over Israel under the authority of King Jesus, and the city of Jerusalem. In Ezekiel 47, we read that a river of fresh water flows up from underneath the temple. It flows west to the Mediterranean Sea and east to the Jordan River where it flows south into the Dead Sea. An abundance of trees will grow on each side of the river, producing fruit every month. Also, the Dead Sea will become fresh water filled with an abundance of fish.

Israel will be the premier nation in the Millennial Kingdom, and Jerusalem will be the capital of the world. King Jesus will reside there and rule the world from there. People from all over the world will come to the Temple to worship the Lord. People will also come to Jerusalem and Israel to study and learn about the Lord and how to be His disciples. Jews will have a heightened knowledge and understanding of scripture. They will teach the Word and share the Gospel with everyone.

IV. Final Battle

At the end of the thousand years, Satan and his demons will be released from the abyss and allowed to deceive the nations one last time. For 1,000 years people will have lived in an ideal kingdom with: 1) an omnipotent king who rules with lovingkindness, justice, and righteousness for the benefit of His subjects; 2) no diseases or aging – perfect health for everyone; 3) prosperity and abundance for all; 4) no crime or lawlessness; 5) righteous officials and judges at every level of government; 6) larger families with no loss of parents or grandparents; etc. In addition, everyone on earth will have heard the Gospel message: that eternal life in heaven with God is available only through faith in Christ and receiving Him as their personal Lord and Savior.

Still, there will be people all over the world who refuse to believe the Gospel message. They will resent having to live under Jesus' rule and obey His laws. They will want to pursue their own sinful desires of lust, greed, power, etc. Satan will be able to deceive these people into thinking they can overthrow Jesus and pursue power and wealth for themselves. Satan will gather all of these rebellious people into a great army and surround Jerusalem.

When the thousand years are completed, Satan will be released from his prison, and will come out to deceive the nations which are in the four corners of the earth, Gog and Magog, to gather them together for the war; the number of them is like the sand of the seashore. And they came up on the broad plain of the earth and surrounded the camp of the saints and the beloved city [Jerusalem], *and fire came down from heaven and devoured them. And the devil who deceived them was thrown into the lake of fire and brimstone, where the beast and the false prophet are also; and they will be tormented day and night forever and ever."*
(Revelation 20:7-10)

This is the final battle where Satan and unrighteous people try to rebel against God. God's victory is decisive as fire falls from heaven to destroy them in the plains surrounding Jerusalem. Following this battle, the Antichrist, the False Prophet, as well as Satan and all his demonic followers, will be in the lake of fire. All of the wicked people who have ever lived are dead. Their souls are in Hades where they are waiting for their final judgment.

CHAPTER 8

FINAL JUDGMENTS

I. Punishment of the Wicked

At the end of the Millennial Kingdom all of those who rejected God and His Christ during their lives throughout the ages will appear before Jesus in what's known as the Great White Throne Judgment.

> *Then I saw a great white throne and Him who sat upon it, from whose presence earth and heaven fled away, and no place was found for them. And I saw the dead, the great and the small, standing before the throne, and books were opened; and another book was opened, which is the book of life* [which includes a list of all the righteous]; *and the dead were judged from the things which were written in the books, according to their deeds. And the sea gave up the dead which were in it, and death and Hades gave up the dead which were in them; and they were judged, every one of them according to their deeds. Then death and Hades were thrown into the lake of fire. This is the second death, the lake of fire. And if anyone's name was not found written in the book of life, he was thrown into the lake of fire."*
> (Revelation 20:11-15)

Note that people are in this judgment because their names are not written in the Book of Life. Thus, they rejected God's offer of redemption during their lifetime. Also, they are all thrown into the lake of fire. However, *"they were judged every one of them according to their deeds"*. This indicates that there are varying degrees of torment in the lake of fire. The person who lived a relatively moral life will not suffer the same as a mass murderer or a false teacher who led many away from Christ. This is consistent with God's character of justice. He will assign to each person a degree of punishment in hell based on their deeds and the choices they made in life.

I'd like to address another point here. Some people believe that this is only a temporary punishment, and that after the wicked have paid for their sins they will be annihilated and cease to exist. That is not scriptural. The Bible teaches that punishment in the lake of fire is everlasting. For example, after Jesus separates the sheep from the goats, He says:

"These will go away into eternal punishment, but the righteous into eternal life." (Matthew 25:46)

The same Greek word for "eternal" is used in both cases; it means "never-ending". So, the punishment of the wicked in the lake of fire will last just as long as believers live in heaven with Christ.

II. **Rewards for the Righteous**

This topic is not described in the scriptures as a one-time event. I decided to place it here because it fits topically, not chronologically.

Those who have confessed and repented of their sins and by faith received Christ as their Savior and Lord are considered righteous before God. Their sins have been dealt with on the cross and will not even be mentioned in this event. Their names are written in "the Book of Life". Therefore, they will rule with Christ in the Millennial Kingdom and live forever with Him in heaven. This is the greatest reward – enjoying a personal relationship with Jesus Christ forever. It is given to us freely; although Jesus paid an infinite price to purchase salvation for us.

Although this judgment is not about going to heaven or hell, the righteous still have to give an account to Jesus for their deeds and the choices they made in life, as Paul summarizes:

> *For we must all appear before the judgment seat of Christ, so that each one may be recompensed for his deeds in the body, according to what he has done, whether good or bad.*
> (II Corinthians 5:10)

This is often referred to as the "Bema Seat" judgment because the Greek word used for "*judgment seat*" is bema. This is not a throne but an elevated platform similar to the one where winners of athletic contests receive their trophies. This process of evaluating the believer's deeds is described by the Apostle Paul in further detail:

> *According to the grace of God which was given to me, like a wise master builder I laid a foundation, and another is building on it. But each man must be careful how he builds on it. For no man can lay a foundation other than the one which is laid, which is Jesus Christ. Now if any man builds on the foundation with gold, silver, precious stones, wood, hay, straw, each man's work will become evident; for the day will show it because it is to be revealed with fire, and the fire itself will test the quality of each man's work. If any man's work which he has built on it remains, he will receive a reward. If any man's work is burned up, he will suffer loss; but he himself will be saved, yet so as through fire.* (I Corinthians 3:10-15)

Basically, this is not a judgment for sin but an evaluation of our deeds for the purpose of earning eternal rewards. For believers in Christ, our sins were paid for by His death on the cross and have been separated from us as far as the east is from the west (Psalm 103:12). In this judgment Jesus will review with us the choices we made and the actions we took throughout our lives. The actions we took that please and honor God and help to build His kingdom for His glory will earn rewards. Actions that we took for our own pleasure or benefit will not earn a reward and will be burned up and forgotten. The rewards may be related to the level of responsibility we have in the Kingdom or in eternity, such as the twelve apostles ruling the twelve tribes of Israel (Matthew 19:28). The Bible also talks about specific crowns awarded to believers for certain behaviors. I expect the rewards will be better than we can ask or imagine and will be personally designed for each individual.

The bottom line is that we are living under a reward system. The choices we make in this life will directly affect the number and quality of rewards that we will enjoy in the Kingdom and in eternity. Everyone will be in heaven because of their faith in Christ, but it is the deeds and choices made in this life that will earn rewards and recognition in heaven.

This concept of rewarding people for their faithful service and choices is a fundamental aspect of God's character:

> *"And without faith it is impossible to please Him, for he who comes to God must believe that He is and that <u>He is a rewarder</u> of those who seek Him."* (Hebrews 11:6)

The question remains: When will this evaluation of the believer's deeds take place? The Bible does not refer to a specific time or place when all believers stand before Christ; therefore, I believe this will happen at different times for different groups. For believers who are caught up in the Rapture, it will occur while we are in heaven during the seven years before we return to earth with

Christ. The Old Testament saints who died before Pentecost and the righteous people who die during the Tribulation will receive their immortal bodies and rewards just before the Millennial Kingdom begins, so they can rule with Christ during the Kingdom. For the righteous people who are alive at the end of the Millennial Kingdom, they will receive their immortal bodies and rewards at that time to prepare them to live with Christ in eternity.

Of course, millions of individual believers could stand before Christ simultaneously, witness the testing of their works privately, receive their rewards, and hear Christ say: "Well done good and faithful servant." This could happen in a moment of time or over an extended time. Christ is not limited by time or space. However, since this is an occasion for Christ to honor His faithful servants, it is more likely to be a celebration with many witnesses.

CHAPTER 9

HEAVEN

After Satan, the demons, and all the wicked people who have ever lived are thrown into the lake of fire, God will eliminate all trace of sin by destroying the current heavens and earth by fire and creating new heavens and a new earth.

> But the day of the Lord will come like a thief, in which the heavens will pass away with a roar and the elements will be destroyed with intense heat, and the earth and its works will be burned up. Since all these things are to be destroyed in this way, what sort of people ought you to be in holy conduct and godliness; looking for and hastening the coming of the day of God, because of which the heavens will be destroyed by burning and the elements will melt with intense heat! But according to His promise we are looking for new heavens and a new earth in which righteousness dwells.
> (II Peter 3:10-13)

God will not just scorch the heavens and earth; He will destroy them down to the elements (atomic components). Then the Lord will create new heavens and a new earth. The prophecy continues:

> Then I saw a new heaven and a new earth; for the first heaven and the first earth passed away, and there is no longer any sea. And I saw the holy city,

new Jerusalem, coming down out of heaven from
God, made ready as a bride adorned for her hus-
band. And I heard a loud voice from the throne,
saying "Behold, the tabernacle of God is among
men, and He will dwell among them, and they
shall be His people, and God Himself will be
among them, and He will wipe away every tear
from their eyes; and there will no longer be any
death; there will no longer be any mourning, or cry-
ing, or pain; the first things have passed away."
And He who sits on the throne said, "Behold, I am
making all things new." (Revelation 21:1-5)

Do you ever wonder what your next home will look
like? Will it be your "forever home" where you will
enjoy your retirement years? Remember that Jesus
told His disciples in John 14:2: "I go to prepare a
place for you." Do you wonder what it will look like?
Well, God has given a detailed description of it in the
book of Revelation. It's a long quote, so I summa-
rized it in my original draft of this book, but my wife
Sandy said, "People need to read this." So, if Christ
is your Savior, this is a description of your real "forever home". Enjoy ...

And he carried me away in the Spirit to a great
and high mountain, and showed me the holy city,
Jerusalem, coming down out of heaven from God,
having the glory of God. Her brilliance was like a
very costly stone, as a stone of crystal-clear jasper. It had a great and high wall, with twelve
gates, and at the gates twelve angels; and names
were written on them [the gates], which are the

names of the twelve tribes of the sons of Israel. There were three gates on the east and three gates on the north and three gates on the south and three gates on the west. And the wall of the city had twelve foundation stones and on them were the twelve names of the twelve apostles of the Lamb.

The one who spoke with me had a gold measuring rod to measure the city, and its gates and its wall. The city is laid out as a square, and its length is as great as the width; and he measured the city with the rod, fifteen hundred miles; its length and width and height are equal. And he measured its wall, seventy-two yards, according to human measurements, which are also angelic measurements. [This is likely the thickness of the wall.] The material of the wall was jasper; and the city was pure gold, like clear glass. The foundation stones of the city wall were adorned with every kind of precious stone. The first foundation stone was jasper; the second, sapphire; the third, chalcedony; the fourth, emerald; the fifth, sardonyx; the sixth, sardius; the seventh, chrysolite; the eighth, beryl; the ninth, topaz; the tenth, chrysoprase; the eleventh, jacinth; the twelfth, amethyst. And the twelve gates were twelve peals; each one of the gates was a single pearl. And the street of the city was pure gold, like transparent glass.

I saw no temple in it, for the Lord God the Almighty and the Lamb are its temple. And the city has no need of the sun or of the moon to shine on *it, for the glory of God has illumined it, and its lamp is the Lamb. The nations will walk by its light, and the kings of the earth will bring their glory into it. In the daytime (for there will be no night there) its gates will never be closed; and they will bring the glory and the honor of the nations into it; and nothing unclean, and no one who practices abomination and lying, shall ever come into it, but only those whose names are written in the Lamb's book of life.* (Revelation 21:10-27)

Yes. There will be "pearly gates" (each one a single massive pearl), and there will be streets of gold. The city is laid out as a cube with its length, width, and height all measuring fifteen hundred miles – more than enough room for the redeemed of all ages to live.

So, the final heavenly state will not involve us sitting on clouds and playing harps. We will be living on earth in a beautiful, spacious city. We will enjoy never-ending fellowship with God Himself and with all the saints who have ever lived. I believe we will also have meaningful work to do, just as God assigned Adam to tend the garden, and we will enjoy the fruits of our labor. It will be much the same as God designed for mankind to live before Adam and Eve sinned.

Chapter 10

Chronological Order of Events

I have described and explained a number of prophetic events in the previous chapters. I thought it would be helpful at this point to summarize the events in the chronological order in which I anticipate they will occur and note the pages in the book where they are discussed.

I. **Rapture of the Church** – could happen at any time (pp. 13-17)

II. **Judgment on Enemies of Israel** – could happen at any time (pp. 19-24)

III. **Seven Years of Tribulation** - (pp. 25-56)

   A. **First 3-1/2 Years** – begins when the Antichrist signs treaty with Israel (pp. 25, 99)

     1. Seal Judgments (pp. 26-29)
     2. The Antichrist gains control over global government and economy. (pp. 40-41, 49)
     3. The False Prophet establishes global religious system. (pp. 39-40, 50-51)

   B. **Midpoint of the Tribulation**

     1. The Antichrist puts an end to the global religious system and the Jewish worship of

God. He demands that he be worshipped as god. (pp. 40, 49, 52)

2. The False Prophet erects a statue of the Antichrist in the temple in Jerusalem and initiates the Mark of the Beast. (pp. 50-52, 100)

3. 144,000 Jewish evangelists are commissioned by God. (page 44)

4. Two prophetic witnesses appear in Jerusalem to proclaim God's judgment and His offer of redemption. (page 44-46)

C. Second 3-1/2 Years

1. Trumpet Judgments (pp. 29-33)
2. Angel flies through heaven proclaiming the Gospel (pp. 46-47)
3. Bowl Judgments (pp. 33-36)
4. At the end, the Antichrist kills the two witnesses, who are then resurrected and rise up to heaven. (page 46)

IV. Second Coming of Christ (pp. 57-64)

A. Jesus and His Church return from heaven to the earth. (pp. 57-61)

B. Jesus annihilates the armies assembled by the Antichrist to prevent His return. (pp. 60-61)

C. The Antichrist and False Prophet are thrown alive into the lake of fire. (pp. 52, 61)

D. Satan and his demons are imprisoned in the abyss for 1,000 years. (page 61)

E. Tribulation martyrs and Old Testament believers are resurrected. (pp. 61-62)
F. Judgment of the Sheep and the Goats determines who will enter alive into the Millennial Kingdom. (pp. 62-64)

V. The Millennial Kingdom (pp. 65-76)

A. Jesus physically rules the world for 1,000 years. (pp. 65-76)
B. At the end of the 1,000 years, Satan is released and gathers all unbelievers to overthrow King Jesus. Fire falls from heaven to destroy them. (pp. 74-76)

VI. Preparation for Eternity

A. Satan and his demons are thrown into the lake of fire. (pp. 75-76)
B. All unbelievers of all ages are resurrected to appear before the Great White Throne Judgment of Christ. They are all thrown into the lake of fire. (pp. 77-78)
C. The current heavens and earth are destroyed by intense heat. (page 83)
D. The holy city, new Jerusalem, comes down from heaven onto the new earth. (pp. 83-86)

VII. The Eternal State

A. The redeemed of all ages will dwell with Christ in the new Jerusalem forever. (pp. 83-86)

B. Those who rejected God from all ages will dwell with Satan in the lake of fire forever. (pp. 63, 77-78)

CHAPTER 11

IF PEOPLE HAVE ALREADY

DISAPPEARED -

WHAT MUST I DO?

If you are reading this book, and the great disappearance (Rapture of the Church) has already taken place, you must be experiencing great fear and confusion. This book can answer many of your questions and let you know what to expect in the near future, and what you can do about it. There are six basic things you need to do:

1. Accept Jesus Christ as your Savior and Lord.
2. Read this book and share it with others.
3. Do <u>NOT</u> take the mark of the beast.
4. Read and study the Bible.
5. Share the Gospel message whenever you can.
6. Identify or develop a network of Christians to help one another during the Tribulation.

I.   Accept Jesus as your Savior and Lord.

As the Bible clearly teaches, all people will live forever; we will not cease to exist when we die or come back in another life. There are only two destinations available after death. Some people will live forever in torment in the lake of fire. Others will live forever in heaven with Jesus. Each person gets to make the decision where they will spend eternity, but we have to make that decision <u>before we die</u>. God makes this clear in the book of Hebrews:

> *...it is appointed for men to die once and after this comes judgment.* (Hebrews 9:27)

If you want to live forever in heaven with Christ, there are a few things you need to know, a decision you have to make, and a prayer you need to pray. It is the most important decision you will <u>ever</u> make (literally).

A. What You Need to Know = THE GOSPEL

The word Gospel literally means "Good News". The good news is that even though your sins have separated you from God, He has provided a way for you to be forgiven and enjoy a personal relationship with Him forever. This is the Gospel message that you need to receive and share with others:

1. God loves you and wants to have a relationship with you.

> *For God so loved the world, that He gave His only begotten Son, that whoever believes in Him shall not perish, but have eternal life.* (John 3:16)

Jesus also said this about Himself:

92

> *I came that they* [you] *might have life and have it abundantly.* (John 10:10)

2. Your sin has separated you from God.

All of us have sinned against God, either through active rebellion against His standards or passive indifference to Him. We know our thoughts, words, and actions are often self-centered and not pleasing or obedient to God. The Bible calls this sin. God is holy and cannot allow sin in His presence. God is also just, and sin must be punished; it cannot just be overlooked. We also can't do enough good deeds to make up for the sins we commit. In God's system of justice, you can't perform acts of community service to pay for your sins. If you break His law, and we all have, you go to prison (hell). This is a real problem for us.

> *...for all have sinned and fall short of the glory of God,* (Romans 3:23)

> *For the wages of sin is death,* [spiritual separation from God], *but the free gift of God is eternal life in Christ Jesus our Lord.* (Romans 6:23)

3. Jesus Christ is God's only provision for your sin problem.

So, the reality is: your sin has separated you from God. If you die in this condition, you will be separated from Him forever in hell. The good news (the Gospel) is that God, through His Son Jesus, provided a way for your sins to be paid for, so you can be with Him forever in heaven. Because Jesus lived a sinless life, His death on the cross can pay the death penalty for your sins.

> *God demonstrates His own love toward us, in that while we were yet sinners, Christ died for us.* (Romans 5:8)

Paul explains that Jesus' substitutionary death satisfies the justice that God's character demands.

> *But now apart from the Law the righteousness of God has been manifested..., even the righteousness of God through faith in Jesus Christ for all those who believe; for there is no distinction; for all have sinned and fall short of the glory of God, being justified as a gift by His grace through the redemption which is in Christ Jesus..., so that He would be just and the justifier of the one who has faith in Jesus.* (Romans 3:21-26)

The term "justified" comes from the Greek word for "righteous". The bottom line is that when we by faith accept Jesus' death on the cross as payment for our sins, and receive Him as our Lord and Savior, God declares us to be righteous.

His resurrection from the dead is proof that Jesus has power over death and that we also can have life after death with Him. His resurrection was documented by the Apostle Paul:

> *Christ died for our sins according to the Scriptures, and that He was buried, and that He was raised on the third day according to the scriptures, and that He appeared to Cephas* [Peter], *then to the twelve* [apostles]. *After that He appeared to more than five hundred brethren at one time, most of whom remain until now, but some have fallen asleep.* [They were still alive when Paul wrote this, so they could have verified or refuted Paul's testimony.]
> (I Corinthians 15:3-6)

There is much evidence that Jesus actually rose from the dead. For me, the strongest evidence is the lives of His disciples. After Jesus was crucified, these men went into hiding, afraid that the authorities would come after them next. Then just a few days later they were in the streets of Jerusalem proclaiming that they had seen him alive and talked to Him. Not only that, but they suffered persecution and many hardships as they traveled extensively proclaiming that Jesus was the Son of God. All but one of these men suffered painful executions, refusing to deny that Jesus rose from the dead. They would not have done that if they knew it to be a lie. No, they had indeed seen Him alive and talked with Him after His crucifixion and burial.

Another critical fact to understand is that Jesus is the only way to God. Jesus Himself clearly declared:

> *I am the way, and the truth, and the life; no one comes to the Father but through me.* (John 14:6)

This is confirmed by Luke in the book of Acts:

> *And there is salvation in no one else, for there is no other name under heaven that has been given among men by which we must be saved.* (Acts 4:12)

There is no Plan B!

B. The Decision You Have to Make

It's not enough just to know these truths. You must personally receive Jesus Christ as your Savior and Lord:

> *As many as received Him, to them He gave the right to become children of God, even to those who believe in His name.* (John 1:12)

To "believe in Him" or "receive Him" means more than just intellectually acknowledging the reality of Christ and understanding the claims of the Gospel. It is acknowledging that Jesus' death on the cross was payment for <u>your</u> sins, and personally accepting this gift from God. It means trust in and personally commit to Christ as your Lord and Savior. The Holy Spirit then enters your life to make you into the person He wants you to be.

Friend, it's decision time for you. You have all the information you need to make your choice. You can decide to accept Jesus' death on the cross as payment for your sins and by faith receive Jesus as your Savior and Lord, or you can decide to remain separated from God by your sins. You have to make the choice and then live with the consequences. Can you imagine living in torment forever knowing that you made the decision today to be there? I would encourage you not to let Satan deceive you into thinking that you can think about it and decide later to receive Christ as your Savior. None of us knows when our life will end, and the decision we made will be final. God in His mercy may choose to give you another chance in the future to receive Jesus and eternal life, but He may not. Make no mistake; a decision to delay making your choice is a decision to reject Jesus today.

...At the acceptable time I listened to you, and on the day of salvation I helped you. Behold, now is "the acceptable time,"

> *behold, now is "the day of salvation" ...*
> (II Corinthians 6:2)

C. The Prayer You Need to Pray

As the Bible affirms, we must receive Christ by faith:

> *For by grace you have been saved through faith; and that not of yourselves, it is the gift of God; not as a result of works, so that no one may boast.* (Ephesians 2:8-9)

If you have decided to receive Christ as your Lord and Savior, all you need to do is tell Him. The words you use are not critical; He who looks on your heart will know your sincerity. You may choose to pray the prayer that I prayed in 1972. It comes from the "Four Spiritual Laws" gospel tract written by Bill Bright (Founder of CRU, formerly Campus Crusade For Christ), Copyright 1965:

"Lord Jesus, I need You. Thank You for dying on the cross for my sins. I open the door of my life and receive You as my Savior and Lord. Thank You for forgiving my sins and giving me eternal life. Take control of the throne of my life. Make me the kind of person You want me to be."

If you sincerely prayed that prayer, then according to God's word you have eternal life right now, and the Holy Spirit dwells in you.

> *And the testimony is this, that God has given us eternal life, and this life is in His Son. He who has the Son has the life; he who does not have the Son of God does not have the life. These things I have written to you who believe in the name of the Son of God, so that you may know that you have eternal life.* (I John 5:11-12)

Congratulations my brother or sister. God has adopted you into His family, and you will live with Him <u>forever</u>!!

II. Read This Book and Share It with Others.

As I shared in the Preface, understanding these prophecies can comfort you and others. It will give hope and assurance that <u>God is in control</u> of the chaotic world around you.

If you are living in the chaos after the great disappearance of millions of people, you will be able to know the exact date when the Antichrist signs the seven-year treaty with Israel that begins the Tribulation period. Exactly 3-1/2 years from that date, the Antichrist will stop the worship of God in the temple in Jerusalem and demand that he be worshipped as god. That will begin the final 3-

1/2 years of the Great Tribulation. At the end of the second 3-1/2 years, Jesus will return to reward His faithful followers, punish the wicked, and set up His kingdom. Signing the treaty with Israel will also definitely identify the Antichrist if he has not yet been revealed. The world leader that signs a seven-year treaty with Israel will be the Antichrist.

III. Do **NOT** Take the Mark of the Beast.

As noted in Chapter 5 (see **The False Prophet**), the Bible sternly warns the followers of Christ not to receive the mark of the beast.

> *If anyone worships the beast and his image and receives a mark on his forehead or on his hand, he also will drink of the wine of the wrath of God, which is mixed in full strength in the cup of His anger; and he will be tormented with fire and brimstone... forever and ever.*
> (Revelation 14:9-11)

This mark will identify the person as a worshipper of the Antichrist and his image. Before taking the mark, each person will have to decide once and for all whom he/she will worship - Jesus Christ or the Antichrist. There will be a cost for refusing to take the mark of the beast, but it will be a temporary cost. (Those who refuse to receive the mark will likely be executed, and then they will spend eternity with Jesus.) Everyone will be required to have this mark to buy or sell anything.

IV. Read and Study the Bible.

If you have access to a Bible, it will be a great re-
source and source of encouragement. If you are
not familiar with the Bible, I recommend you start
by reading the book of John to learn who Jesus
really is. Then read through the rest of the New
Testament to learn more about Jesus and how He
wants us to live today. Finally, if you have time,
read through the Old Testament to learn about
God the Father and how He has dealt with mankind in the past. Many end time prophecies are
found in the Old Testament.

V.   Share the Gospel.

Share the Gospel message (the Good News given
in Section I of this chapter) whenever you can.
Historically, the church has always been strongest and grown fastest when it was persecuted. It
will be the same during the Tribulation period.
People will be living in terror and looking for any
hope that things will get better. The Gospel will
give them hope and will give them a chance to
spend eternity in heaven rather than hell.

VI.   Join a Community of Believers.

As the seven years of Tribulation begin, Christians and Jews will experience increasing levels of
persecution. This will come from government
agencies, friends, strangers, and even family

members. This will become acute for those who refuse to receive the mark of the beast. In every nation in the past where the church has been persecuted, underground churches and networks have formed for mutual support and encouragement. It will be important for you to join such a community of believers or start one.

When the Rapture occurs, there will be mass confusion as everyone tries to figure out what happened. This will be the best time to share the truth with others because you will be one of the few people who really knows what happened. As others respond to the truth and receive Christ as their Savior, start forming networks of believers before the persecution begins.

CHAPTER 12

IF THE RAPTURE HASN'T

HAPPENED YET -

HOW SHOULD I LIVE?

In the past there have been individuals who have predicted the time, some even the day, when Jesus was going to return. In some cases, people quit their jobs, sold their homes, and gathered together to wait for the anticipated return. I certainly would not advocate anything like that, but I think it would be wise to consider that He might return soon and live accordingly.

In Matthew 24, Jesus's disciples asked Him an interesting question:

> Tell us, when will these things happen, and what will be the sign of Your coming, and of the end of the age? (Matthew 24:3)

We have discussed much of His answer, but this is how He addressed the question of timing:

> Now learn the parable from the fig tree: when its branch has already become tender and puts forth its leaves, you know that summer is near; so, you too, when you see all these things, recognize that He is near, right at the door...But of that day and hour no one knows, not even the angels of heaven,

*nor the Son, but the Father alone.... Therefore, be
on the alert, for you do not know which day your
Lord is coming.... **For this reason you also must
be ready; for the Son of Man is coming at an
hour when you do not think He will**.*
(Mathew 24:32-44)

So, what would it look like to "*be ready*"? There are
differing opinions as to the interpretation and timing
of end time prophecies, but in all cases, there should
be the same sense of urgency for personally accepting Jesus Christ as Savior and Lord and for sharing
the gospel with others.

The first and most important thing to do is to **Accept
Jesus as Your Savior and Lord.** If you are not sure
whether or not you are a redeemed child of God,
please read **Chapter 11, Section I** of this book. I
suggest you go there right now and read through this
first key step. It discusses the most important decision you will ever make in your life, which will affect
the quality of your life on earth and in eternity. After
you deal with that critical issue, come back here and
continue.

Returning to the question of what it would look like
to "*be ready*", I would say: Don't stop living your life,
but live it well! Throughout Scripture we are encouraged to walk before God in humility and the fear of
the Lord. This must be a vital part of any plan to "*be
ready*". The key to humility is developing a heart of
gratefulness. As we remember that God and others
have invested in us to help us become who we are
today, it helps us to maintain humility. The fear of

the Lord is also commended throughout scripture. It involves turning from evil and doing good. (Psalm 34:11-14 and Proverbs 3:7 are examples.)

We find another perspective on what it means to "*be ready*" in the book of Micah.

> *He has told you, O man, what is good; and what does the LORD require of you but to do justice, to love kindness, and to walk humbly with your God?* (Micah 6:8)

Having confirmed that you are a redeemed child of God, the next most important thing to do is to **Develop Your Personal Relationship with God.** It's difficult to have a relationship with someone unless you spend time with them. There are three things that will help you develop your personal relationship with God:

1. Study His word. God has revealed Himself to us in the Bible. In the Old Testament we learn about God the Father – how He created the universe from nothing and how He related to mankind before the birth of Jesus. In the Old Testament we also learn about His character, values, emotions, divine attributes, and His heart. In the New Testament we learn about God the Son and God the Holy Spirit. We learn about God's mercy, grace, and justice as Jesus died on the cross to redeem us. We also learn a great deal in the New Testament about how He wants us to live and relate to Him and other people.

2. Spend time alone with God each day to develop an intimate, personal relationship with Him. This would involve talking and listening to Him, as well as studying His word. It is helpful to have a quiet place where you can meet with God every day at the same time. Make this a high priority in your schedule, and it will become a priority and a habit that you will not want to miss.

3. Join and/or develop a community of committed Christians who are growing in their relationship with God. The best way to do this is to join a local church where the Bible is taught and people are growing in their relationship with God. As you get involved in the ministries of the church, you will develop friendships with others who will encourage you in your walk with Christ. You may also identify believers at work, school, your neighborhood, or other arenas. You could initiate a Bible study or other activities in order to encourage each other to grow as disciples of Christ. Inviting nonbelievers to join the group would be a great way to share the Gospel in a winsome way.

There is a lot of talk these days about "Finishing Well", but none of us knows when our life will end. The only way to guarantee that we will finish well is to live well and love well every day, in whatever season of life or circumstance we find ourselves. I love the expression: "Living with the end in mind." Someday I will stand before Jesus and give an account of the choices I've made in my life. It could be today. I need to live each day with that reality in mind; I need to be faithful today.

The book of Titus offers the motivation and prescription for living well as a follower of Christ:

For the grace of God has appeared, bringing salvation to all men, instructing us to deny ungodliness and worldly desires and to live sensibly, righteously, and godly in the present age, looking for the blessed hope and the appearing of the glory of our great God and Savior, Christ Jesus, who gave Himself for us to redeem us from every lawless deed, and to purify for Himself a people for His own possession, zealous for good deeds. (Titus 2:11-14)

ONE FINAL THOUGHT

Thus says the Lord, "Let not a wise man boast of his wisdom, and let not the mighty man boast of his might, let not a rich man boast of his riches; but let him who boasts boast of this, that he understands and knows Me, that I am the Lord who exercises lovingkindness, justice and righteousness on earth; for I delight in these things," declares the Lord. (Jeremiah 9:23-24)

This is one of my favorite scripture passages because it reveals the heart of God. He wants His children to know Him. Even deeper He wants us to understand Him. This requires us to spend time with Him in His word where He reveals Himself. As a father, and now a grandfather, I want to have a relationship with my children and grandchildren. I don't want them to just know about me, but to know me, love me, and enjoy spending time with me. Likewise, I want to know them, understand them, and spend time with them. I want to share with them things that I've learned to help them have a fruitful life and avoid mistakes that I've made.

As a man with very limited knowledge and understanding and an active sin nature, I have only a glimpse of the infinite love that God has for His children. The sovereign creator and ruler of the universe loves me unconditionally, redeemed me by dying on a cross for my sins, placed His Holy Spirit in me, promised to never leave me or forsake me and to cause all things to work together for my good. Now He invites me to "understand and know" Him personally. <u>How could I refuse?</u> Since the Lord brought these verses to my attention years ago, I have made it my life goal to understand and know Him more deeply as the years go by.

In this book I have focused on the time that is coming when God will exercise His final justice and righteousness on the earth as He puts an end to all evil and wickedness in the universe. However, as this verse indicates, the first desire of God's heart is to exercise lovingkindness on the earth, especially to His children. We will experience that in part in this life and then in full in the Millennial Kingdom and in Eternity.

I want to leave you with one last precious promise that gives another glimpse into our Father's heart. It assures us that we cannot comprehend or even imagine the blessings God has prepared for us.

> *...Things which eye has not seen and ear has not heard, and which have not entered the heart of man, **all that God has prepared for those who love Him**."* (I Corinthians 2:9)

If you have any questions or comments after reading this book, I would love to hear from you. You may contact me at **Bill@Freeman611.com** .

Be Blessed, My Friend,

Bill Freeman